IN THIS HILARIOUS AND HEARTFELT BOOK, A FATHER TAKES A BREAK
FROM EVERY GUY'S DREAM GIG—COVERING FOOTBALL (AND THE ODD
SWIMSUIT SHOOT) FOR *SI*—TO GIVE IT A GO AS MR. MOM.

After nineteen years as a writer for *Sports Illustrated*, Austin Murphy
should have had it made. Instead, he'd had it—with clumsy wandings
of recently federalized airline security agents; with measuring his life
by hotel rooms and Heisman stories; with the members of his church
assuming that his wife, Laura, was a single mother. With each missed
birthday, recital, and play, he became more convinced that he was
missing out on his kids' lives.

So he decided to trade in his current job for a new one: Laura's.
Once an ambitious young journalist, Laura had backburnered her career
when she went on the mommy track. Now, with a "wife" of her own,
she would be able to write full time, while he could be present for more
Kodak moments.

Alas, the man charged with preparing three nutritious meals a day
had never mastered his own outdoor grill. And that was just the beginning. Sublimely ignorant of everything from grocery shopping, to
housecleaning, to the need to trim his children's nails more than, say,
semiannually, Murphy embarked on his journey much as Shackleton
took on the Southern Ocean: spectacularly ill-equipped to survive it.
Between the lice checks, the spring break trip to Las Vegas, and the
chairmanship of the Lower Brookside Elementary Variety Show, there
were bound to be casualties.

Lively, poignant, and laugh-out-loud funny, *How Tough Could It Be?*
is the story of one man's decision to reorder his life around things that
really matter, and of his adventures (and misadventures) along the way.

ALSO BY AUSTIN MURPHY

The Sweet Season

How Tough Could It Be?

How Tough Could It Be?

THE TRIALS AND ERRORS
OF A SPORTSWRITER
TURNED STAY-AT-HOME DAD

AUSTIN MURPHY

HENRY HOLT AND COMPANY • NEW YORK

Henry Holt and Company, LLC
Publishers since 1866
115 West 18th Street
New York, New York 10011

Henry Holt® is a registered trademark of
Henry Holt and Company, LLC.

Library of Congress Cataloging-in-Publication Data
ISBN: 0-8050-7480-5

Henry Holt books are available for special promotions and
premiums. For details contact: Director, Special Markets.

First Edition 2004

Designed by Kelly S. Too

Printed in the United States of America

1 3 5 7 9 10 8 6 4 2

To Patricia Reeves Murphy,
The best there ever was

Contents

How Tough Could It Be?

Introduction

My story begins at the end, on the last play of the final game of the 2002 college football season. At 10:17 on a cool night in the desert, I stood fifteen yards from Miami quarterback Ken Dorsey in double overtime on the final snap of the national championship game. From my vantage, six feet beyond the end zone in the Fiesta Bowl, I could read Dorsey's eyes as he dropped back to pass, could see a blitzing linebacker get a hand on his collar and spin him like a rag doll. I watched Dorsey's desperation pass fall harmlessly to the turf, sealing Ohio State's first national title in thirty-four years.

There was Maurice Clarett in the bedlam on the field afterward, drained and complaining, "Man, this shit be too long." There were the other Buckeyes, ripping open bags of Tostitos, tossing the contents skyward, covering the heads and shoulders of innocent bystanders with what appeared to be enormous flakes of dandruff.

There was Buckeye head coach Jim Tressel, dapper in his trademark sweater vest, shouting into a microphone, "We've always had the best damn band in the land"—nice in-rhyme, Jim—"and now we've got the best damn *team* in the land."

The guy to whom I found myself drawn, oddly enough, was one of Tressel's assistants—offensive coordinator Jim Bollman, a gruff and mustachioed old lineman whom I'd interviewed a few times over the years. Bollman's wife and two daughters had found their way down to the field, where they joyously embraced him. They clung to one another, not saying anything, just sobbing for joy. It was quite poignant; I was tearing up as well.

But the moment passed, and I found myself swept up in the post–title game carnival. The next twenty-four hours were a blur of hotel rooms and interviews, one of which involved riding around for nine holes in a golf cart with Buckeyes quarterback Craig Krenzel. When I wasn't asking him about key plays in the game, I raked a couple of traps for the guy. It seemed like the least I could do.

Two days after the Fiesta Bowl I found myself thinking back to the Bollmans. I was cross-legged on the floor in my house, flipping through the family photo albums, gazing at snapshots and wondering, picture after picture: Where the hell was I? Where was Dad for this Fourth of July celebration? (Covering a rodeo in Arkansas, naturellement.) Why no Dad at Willa's baptism? (I showed up a half hour late, having been dispatched to Los Angeles on short notice the night before—the day of O.J.'s white Bronco chase—to stake out Al Cowlings' apartment.) Where was I during this Easter egg hunt, this birthday party, this weekend at the Sea Ranch? Where was I on New Year's Eve?

Oh yeah. I was in Knoxville that weekend. Or Calgary or Corvallis or Ann Arbor. I was at the Orange Bowl. I was stuck in O'Hare. No wonder I was drawn to other people's Kodak moments. I was nowhere to be found in most of my own.

I was in my nineteenth year writing for *Sports Illustrated*. It was a pretty sweet job, overall. In addition to a couple of years on the NHL and a fair amount of reporting for the swimsuit issue, my main beats have been college and pro football. That's a lot of leathery-faced men feeding me not just insipid boilerplate but *redundant* insipid boilerplate: *That was a heckuva football game . . . They're a great football team . . . That Roy Williams is a heckuva football player.* (How about this, Coach: Unless you specify a different game, I'll just assume we're talking about football.) But I'm nitpicking. There are some great people on the football beat. My wife, Laura, gives me periodic grief because I have only a few good friends (all right, one friend) in our hometown in northern California. If you came on the road with me, I tell her, you'd feel the love. I've got friends in press boxes and coach's offices all over the country.

The only downside to this gig—aside from the soulless bean counters who vetted my expense reports and the geniuses who decided we should merge with AOL—was the travel: I'd been on the road for half of my marriage and half of my children's lives. Sitting there with those photo albums, testaments to my chronic absenteeism, I reached my own personal tipping point.

IT'S NOT LIKE I WAS SAUL, STRUCK BY LIGHTNING ON THE ROAD to Damascus. This feeling had been building for a while. Almost a year earlier, I'd had a kind of watershed conversation with Laura. Having come home long enough to do a couple loads of laundry following the '01 football season, I'd flown to Hawaii for a story on surf god Kelly Slater, then to Utah for the Winter Olympics, then to Los Angeles to immortalize a Pac-10 power forward with a 1.9 GPA. I was finally back in my own bed, alongside my beloved, who happened upon an ad for a cooking school in Provence while skimming through the *New Yorker*.

"Wouldn't this be great," she said. "We could both go, and I could write an essay on your misadventures with whisks and knives.

"Of course I could never get anyone to assign it," she continued, "because I've been too busy cooking your meals and raising your goddam children."

She said it with a smile on her face and a serrated edge in her voice. Back in 1985, when we started dating, both of us were ambitious young journalists on separate tracks to conventional success. Sixteen years later, because of biology, basically, I was farther up the track. My working day was spent writing. On a good day she *might* spend half her day writing. As a semi-single mother whose spouse was out of town half the year, Laura Hilgers, who'd taken my hand in marriage but not my name, had back-burnered her career in order to raise the kids and run the household. Thus did she spend her life balancing orthodontist appointments with interviews of CEOs and university professors. Our system was set up to guarantee Laura's exhaustion and frustration, which was set up to guarantee my exhaustion.

It wasn't fair. Nor, I used to think to myself, was it my problem. Confronted with the injustice of our equation, I would automatically tender this hollow offer: "Hey, anytime you wanna trade places . . ."

Easy to say when you know it'll never happen.

But that evening, registering the combined desperation and anger in Laura's voice and the fatigue in my own, I noticed that the reflexive offer didn't feel so hollow. I was as sick of living in hotels as Laura was of saying good-bye to me, then backing into that doomed, one-on-two zone defense against the children, a pair of worthy adversaries named Willa and Devin. She is an eight-year-old who reads voraciously and picks at her food. He is a seventy-five-pound six-year-old who eats voraciously—"I told you I needed three eggs," he admonished me on a recent morning, when I'd fried only two—and picks his nose. Willa's precocious intellect manifests itself in her reading habits (she has gone through each book in the J. K. Rowling oeuvre at least six times) and an elevated grasp of ethics. On those rare occasions when I let slip a blast of profanity, she will ask me, rhetorically, "Why do you think Devin uses those words?" His precocity is limited mainly to his size, strength, and, as suggested above, sporadic use of adult language. Every week these two evolved further into their distinct and delightful personalities. It was getting tougher, not easier, to leave them.

IN COVERING THE OLYMPICS, THE SUPER BOWL, THE TOUR DE France, I'd always told myself that I was drawing the marrow from life. *This is so awesome! I'm sitting in a café in the Loire Valley, shooting the shit with Lance Armstrong!*

Of late, however, a competing voice in my head never failed to remind me, as I bobbed on a boat at a surf contest off the coast of Sumatra or sat in a nightclub with Warren Sapp, that I might be having fun, feeding my ego, but I wasn't living life to the fullest. In fact, I was missing the most important part of it. *You are husband to a gorgeous woman and father to her two young children,* I would think. *Get your ass home.*

What brings a loyal employee to this point? There was no cathartic, expletive-bomb-laced screaming match with an editor. No one had delivered a huge overhand right that put me on the canvas—*We're switching you back to hockey*—and into this frame of mind. I'd been driven to it, rather, by countless body shots, a hundred minor heartbreaks. The phone rings on Monday and I start packing. I'm needed in Milwaukee for the Frozen Four; in Houston for PGA golf; Nebraska for—what else?—Cornhusker football.

After digesting the news, Laura might let slip a brief protest—*You realize you're going to miss Willa's birthday, again*—then fall silent, ever the good soldier. She knew the drill. This was how we paid the mortgage. These were our lives. As a senior writer at *SI*, I measured out my existence in deadlines, hotel rooms, and Heisman stories. I was a virtual husband to my wife and a virtual father to my children, who despite their tender years were already disinclined to take my calls from the road, so predictable had my questions become: *How was school today? What moves did you learn in karate? Which pajamas are you wearing?*

The fractured plans, the disappointments, and the odd number of members at our family outings (people at our church assumed, after a while, that Laura was a single mother) piling up over the years had at last achieved a kind of critical mass. I was not just missing my children's birthdays and recitals and plays, I realized. I was missing their lives. I would not get a chance to do this over.

How to reclaim some of that time? How to fight my way back

into my own photo albums? How about if I traded places with their mother? How tough could it be?

I wasn't about to let a few inconvenient facts—I can't cook, can be quick to anger, never owned a day planner, never quite got in the habit of balancing a checkbook—come between me and what I foresaw, naively, as a prolonged idyll in the bosom of family. We were *owed* this time together, is the way I saw it. Sitting there on the floor that January morning, I took inventory. Laura needed a wife, and I needed an excuse to stay home for a good long while.

THAT NIGHT IT WAS DECIDED. HAVING PUT THE CHILDREN TO BED, we agreed to flip-flop. I would assume Laura's duties—whatever they were—while she flung herself into her long-neglected writing career. She would kiss me good-bye each morning and head to the office.

How long could this go on? That was a dicey one. I was afraid that if I asked for a year's leave from *SI,* my bosses might say, "You know what, Murph? Why stop at a year? Why not take the rest of your career off?"

The arrangement would last six months, we decided. I worried, at the time, that a half year was too little time at home. "I think you'll find," Laura assured me, "that the days won't pass as quickly as you think they will. Once you agree to do this," she said, an ominous tone in her voice, "there can be no turning back."

At the time, I thought she was being a trifle melodramatic. I see now, looking back, that I was merely ignorant. I didn't know what I didn't know.

———

I CALLED MY BOSSES AT *SI* AND ASKED FOR SOME TIME OFF. NOT because I didn't love the job, I assured them; I did. But I also happened to be fond of my wife, and the children we'd brought into this world. I felt like spending more than, say, four uninterrupted days with them at a time. I wanted to go at least half a year without making that sad drive to the airport, there to raise my arms for zealous, dim-witted, and recently federalized airline security agents, who would wand me vigorously, then point toward my groin and say, "I'm going to pat you in this area; is that okay?"

I would be the world's happiest SAHD (Stay-at-Home Dad). I'd cook, carpool, fold laundry, and find out how it feels to be, well, Laura. I would volunteer in the classroom and arrange playdates. I'd do the grocery shopping and pick up the dry cleaning. I would befriend and gossip with the other mommies, taking care, if I must ogle them, to be discreet about it. I'd accept the thanks of Laura, whose own career, thanks to my selflessness, would take wing. And when she moved in close, late of a weekday evening, the better to express her gratitude, I would borrow a page from her playbook. Professing exhaustion, I'd withhold sex.

As it happened, my longing to swap duties with my wife dovetailed with a national trend. "Nobody has measured how widespread this phenomenon is," according to *Fortune*'s cover story on October 14, 2002, "Trophy Husbands." "But there is clearly a dramatic shift afoot."

"Call him what you will," the story reads, "Househusband, stay-at-home-dad, domestic engineer. But credit him with setting aside his own career . . . so that's his wife's career might flourish and their family might thrive."

———

———

THE IDEA, HALF-BAKED AS IT WAS AT THE TIME, WAS THAT I'D punch the clock for the magazine for a few more months, then ease into the Mr. Mom role in, say, August.

You can have your leave of absence, came the word from *SI*. But you'll need to start in two weeks.

I walked from the office to the kitchen, where Laura was making herself some lunch. She smiled as I delivered the news, then immediately went into drill sergeant mode:

"You'll need a day planner, and you'll need to get in the habit of writing things on the calendar. Do you know where the calendar is?

"We'll need to sit down and go over the finances. You realize that if you screw this up, the bank will foreclose on our house.

"Look on my desk for the HomeChef catalog. There may still be time for you to sign up for cooking lessons . . ."

"I need you to start noticing their nails."

GAME ON. PRIVATE MURPHY, REPORTING FOR DUTY.

———

Pregame

I embark on this journey spectacularly ill-equipped to survive it. The man who will be asked to prepare three nutritious meals a day has never used his own outdoor grill ("ignitor" button issues). The family finances are about to become the responsibility of one who forks over at least a hundred bucks a year in fees for bounced checks in his personal account. Organization, patience, discipline—common traits in successful housewives—are not strong suits of mine.

What then, are my strong suits? I'm a quick study. For a guy in his early forties, I'm in good shape. I've got some stamina. The way I see it it, I can do this thing—as soon as someone will tell me what it is. I am like most husbands. We think we have a vague idea of what our wives do in our absence, if we think about it all. We seldom wonder, or ask, how the house got clean or how the fridge got filled. But our feelings are hurt when our spouses fail to lavish praise on us for putting a new roll of toilet paper on the dispenser when the old one runs out.

So I pose the question that has offended housewives down through the ages: What do you do all day?

It is the query that doubles as a contraceptive, often precluding the possibility of conjugal relations for up to a week. When I ask Laura now, however, she knows that what I mean is, What would *I* do all day, if I were you?

She seems glad I've asked. The next day I am presented with—have thrust under my nose, in fact—a twenty-three-point memo that starts with "make breakfasts, lunches, and dinners" and ends with "write all cards (Christmas) and notes (thank you, congratulations, condolence)." A sampling of onerous duties in between:

Plan a weekly menu and do grocery shopping. Whoa. Who thinks about what they're going to be eating six days from now? Laura, apparently. Of course, having all those victuals in the house won't do me much good until I . . .

Learn to cook a real meal that I can eat (includes getting all the parts on the table at the same time). Note the phrase "real meal," chosen to exclude my specialties: omelets, grilled cheese sandwiches, canned soup. Plus, she wants it served all at once. Has she ever heard of crawling before you can walk?

Tidy house every day—really tidy. This is a strife generator. "Really tidy"? Whose definition of tidy are we going by?

Arrange playdates. The trick here, I will learn, is getting both kids invited to different playdates at the same time.

No television. Clearly she does not mean for this to be construed literally.

Finances: maybe you should keep the checkbook, maybe not. Have I mentioned that Laura is really smart?

Keep track of when the kids need baths. That's an easy one: they're in constant need of baths. Under the care of Goodwife Murphy, they can expect maybe three a week.

Laundry: fold it and put it away THE SAME DAY. What we've got going on here is a woman setting the bar higher for me than she does for herself.

Read all of the school information and respond to it. Simple enough. Let's just rummage through the recycling bin and extract the bulletin from Mrs. Bishop, Devin's kindergarten teacher. They need volunteers for next Monday's lice check. (On second thought, maybe the kids need four baths a week.)

Plan and execute birthday parties. How about if, instead, I execute those responsible for transforming children's birthday parties from what they were to what they are? Back in the day, it was pin-the-tail-on-the-donkey, a piñata if you were lucky; then cake, presents, and see ya later, kiddies, don't let the door hit you in the ass on your way out. Celebrations are now required to rival, in extravagance and expense, a collaboration between David Wolper and Sir Richard Attenborough.

Stay ahead of minor house repairs. That's self-evident, and a bit of a cheap shot, included on the list because it took me longer than Laura liked—maybe a month—to make it down to the hardware store to replace the cracked toilet seat. (She disapproved of my stopgap solution: a band of duct tape that didn't exactly shout *House Beautiful* but that did put an end to the serial bun-pinchings.)

What will I talk about with the repair guys? It should make for an interesting dynamic: I'll stand at the kitchen counter, distributing pink sprinkles on the cookies for the Valentine's Day party, while they wander the house, tool belts pulling their dungarees low in back as they think to themselves, *What's this loser's story?*

I can expect to feel a trifle emasculated, according to a research paper I found posted on Slowlane.com, a Web site devoted to stay-at-home Dads. All but the most thick-skinned SAHDs are in for a rough go, writes Laura Cobb, a professor of child development and family studies at Purdue University: "Nontraditional expressions of gender arouse suspicion and leave men vulnerable to negative societal repercussions. The man who crosses over into a female-dominated area upsets the gender assumptions embedded in 'women's work.' Almost immediately they are suspected of not being a 'real man.' "

The way I see it, with all due respect to Dr. Cobb, the man who crosses over into a female-dominated area finds himself hip-deep in females, in a primo position to check them out and chat them up. It is no reflection on my rock-solid relationship with Laura that I might actually enjoy mingling with some of these Marin County MILFs. (While I am not certain what that acronym stands for, I have deduced, from the contexts in which I've heard men use it, that it must mean, "Mothers I'd Like to Frisk" or "Mothers Indisputably Looking Fine" or, possibly, "Mothers with whom I'd Like to discuss the Federalist papers.")

———

THE COOKING DUTIES DAUNT ME MORE THAN ANY OTHER. A WEEK before Laura and I officially trade places, I decide to make a family dinner, maybe get some rookie mistakes out of my system. What the hell: if Grandma Moses didn't get serious about painting until her mid-seventies, who's to say I can't pick up cooking at forty-one?

The journey of a thousand miles begins, in this case, with a short walk to our herb garden, where I snip a healthy sprig from a clump of thyme growing outside the door of our home office. Who knew we had an herb garden? When Laura points the thyme out to me, I allow as how, if I'd known it was an herb, I wouldn't have dumped leftover coffee on it most afternoons for the last few years.

The recipe I'm following calls for the thyme to be inserted into—it seems vulgar, un*sensual,* to write "shoved up"—the cavity of the four-pound roasting chicken. By the time I get the onion and garlic heads cut and "strewn" about the pan and the bird buttered, salted, peppered, and plugged, it is 4:30. Before so much as opening the oven door, I've already committed my most grievous error. The fowl still has to roast for two hours at 375 degrees. The children are accustomed to dining at 5:30, and are invariably surly with hunger a half hour before that. By postponing their nourishment, I have ensured that our home will ring, in the very near future, with their shrill lamentations. A chronology of the entropy that follows:

4:34: Devin asks me if he can have a Milky Way, one of the last surviving treats from his Halloween predations. He has

———

difficulty enunciating the request, having already stuffed the bar into his mouth.

"KinnovuMikWum?" is how it comes out.

"Yes, you can, and thanks for first securing my permission," I reply. Laura says the kids don't get sarcasm, but I hold out hope.

4:44: My brother Matt phones from Colorado. While dicing Yukon Gold potatoes, I share my predicament with him: the kids are ravenous, and dinner's still 105 minutes away. "Crank the oven up to, like, four seventy-five," he says, "and it'll be done in half the time. That's what I'd do." Thanks a shitload, Matt.

Laura will be home from the health club in half an hour, by which time I want to have the potatoes in the oven and the counter wiped down. (It is an unseemly riot of congealed butter, butcher paper, garlic skin, and onion leavings.) I want to convey the illusion that I am master of the situation, but the situation keeps intruding. While I roust Spike, our standard poodle, from the garbage bin—he is frantic to get at the little bag of giblets, with which I could not be bothered—the still-hungry Devin climbs onto the kitchen counter, where he forages like Yogi Bear through the cabinets.

"Devin, get the hell off the counter," I say.

"I'm telling Mommy you said the H-word," he says, descending with a packet of taco shells. Rather than acknowledge guilt, the lad goes on the offensive: "Why do we have taco shells if Mommy never makes tacos?"

I advise him to take that up with her when he is finished narking on me.

5:03: Potatoes now roasting beneath bird. Before making salad, I will unload the dishwasher, in order to begin filling it. My purpose: to prove to Laura that it is possible to prepare a meal and clean up after yourself as you go.

It is a source of profound disappointment to my wife that I remain a willful ignoramus in the kitchen, a culinary philistine whose taste buds, as she sometimes informs me, "are in your ass." Early in our marriage, she'd held out hope that I might evolve into the kind of person who, like her, thought that hanging around the kitchen with one's partner, sipping a hearty Merlot and preparing a meal, was a marvelous way to while away an afternoon. Despite minor improvements, I have remained, on the whole, an adrenaline addict who would rather spend that afternoon biking on Mount Tamalpais. I have made such halting, paltry progress toward her ideal that Laura is finding it increasingly difficult to conceal her bitterness. Because our rule is that whoever cooks doesn't have to clean, she has punished me every time she's stepped into the kitchen by dirtying as many pots, pans, knives, whisks, spoons, and spatulae as possible.

5:20: Devin is "helping" me make the salad by tearing leaves from a head of lettuce and a smaller, denser head of radicchio. He misidentifies the latter as "ridiculo," a sublime malaprop that could double as an adjective for the sad and ancient salad spinner we are filling. When the spinner's plastic outer shell cracked a couple of years ago, I repaired it with duct tape. Somehow, we've never gotten around to replacing it (tape or salad spinner). The tape peels back a tiny bit each time the spinner is washed, serving as a reminder of how hopelessly, pathetically we are trailing in the Game of Life, and exposing us, with each salad made, to minute amounts of duct-tape adhesive.

If it's not adhesive, it's . . . traces of water-based Crayola paint. When the time comes to slap the melted butter onto the bird, I search frantically for several minutes for the pastry brush (it is broken, I will discover, and hasn't been replaced), then grab one of the kids' paintbrushes from the art supply cabinet. I rinse the hell out of it, then get to work. The butter stays yellow. It's all good.

5:39: Laura returns from the Body Pump class. She does not seem to notice, or care, that the counter is wiped down, the dishwasher unloaded, the carrots peeled and sliced. What she does notice is that I am running roughly an hour behind, that I have used butter on the chicken, even though she is allergic to dairy (she'd suggested I substitute olive oil for butter; I'd forgotten), and that neither of the children have been bathed.

"But thank you for making dinner," she says.

It seems like a lot of work for six words of praise. I must always remember: I am not doing this for Laura's approval. I am doing it to find out what it feels like to live in her world, to learn valuable skills and lessons such as: What Happens When Young Children Are Not Fed Dinner on Time.

5:55: They undergo cataclysmic, Old Testament meltdowns, such as the collapse suffered by Willa, who had been reading on the sofa in the living room until choosing this moment to cast her Lemony Snicket book on the floor and sob, "I'm hungry!" After intense negotiations—Would she like Chee-tos? *Hellll* no. "I like the puffy ones but you always get the skinny kind!" she accuses, bitterly—she agrees to accept buttered toast and a glass of milk.

6:02: As Laura showers and I prepare Willa's snack, a suspicious growling emanates from Spike's crate. Funny, I don't remember incarcerating the dog. Closer inspection reveals a crate occupied by Spike and a certain six-year-old. They are having a little taco-shell picnic. I reach down to open the gate, latched from the inside by Devin, then think better of it. What we are killing here, with dog and boy in self-imposed captivity, is two birds with one stone.

6:15: I turn my attention to the recipe. The matter of the reduction sauce has hung over my head these past hours like the sword of Damocles. As if cooking the friggin' bird weren't enough, the recipe calls for "½ cup dry white wine or vermouth" and "4 cups chicken stock" and "1 tablespoon gelatin." When the chicken is done, I'm supposed to "pour off the fat, add stock and optional gelatin and reduce to about half by vigorous boiling."

With the hour late and the children in open mutiny, this added task is weighing heavily. Sensing my despair, Laura calls out, from the bathroom, "I *never* do the reduction sauce. If I were you I'd skip the whole thing." I want to kiss her, and not just because she is standing there in nothing but a towel.

6:33: I am at the ready with oven mitts as the timer finally beeps. The chicken smells wonderful and looks good. "You got the breast side up!" says Laura. This is like the football coach congratulating his worst player for successfully buckling his chin strap, but I'll take compliments where I can get them.

The potatoes disappoint. They seem spongy and under-done. Laura explains that I should not have placed them beneath the chicken—it affects the distribution of heat in the oven.

"But don't worry," she says, poking one of the tubers with

a fork. "I mean, it's not like they're not edible." Over the next half year, we will come to know from inedible.

Helping herself to a leg-thigh, she pays me a more valuable compliment: "Do you see how it comes apart at the joints like that? That's good. A well-roasted chicken basically yields itself up to you."

Once they've got a few mouthfuls of chicken in them, the kids are no longer dueling Antichrists. They're our kids again. Which means I must ask Willa to *pass* her unwanted chicken skin to her brother, rather than flinging it across the table as one would toss food to a zoo animal.

Having prepared the meal, I am more inclined to come down hard on food tossing and to make sure napkins are on laps. I feel proprietary ownership of the event. The rewards for my labors transcend the fact that, on this one night, someone else will have to do the dishes. I find myself taking pleasure in the sight of my loved ones savoring fare I've prepared for them. It is a kind of gastronomical Sally Field moment: *They like it! They really like it!*

I take more pleasure in the food myself. I chew more slowly. I can taste the tiny bite of the thyme; I can see how it works in the recipe. And while I never got around to the reduction sauce, I am able to find a use for the wine.

Here is the real payoff: Laura can't stop complimenting me and thanking me. In this regard, it turns out, Laura is like a well-roasted chicken. Cook for her, and she becomes ever so slightly more inclined to yield herself up to you.

SUPER BOWL SUNDAY IS MR. MOM EVE. THE DAY BEFORE I MAKE it official, Coach Laura accompanies me to the grocery store.

Not just any grocery store. There is a Safeway about six hundred yards from our house, but do we do our shopping there? Of course not. That would be far too easy, and far less holistic. Laura, you see, has food issues, not to be confused with eating issues. The woman puts away more grub than I do. On our first dinner date, when I reached across the table to spear a morsel from her plate—surely a sylph such as herself wouldn't be finishing her entire entrée!—she parried my fork with her own. "Back off," she said. For the last seventeen years, I have.

By food issues, I mean she is allergic to, I think, all but four or five foods in the world. Basically, she can eat meat and vegetables—and not all vegetables. Since she went on this outlandishly spartan diet, the insomnia that plagued her for twenty years has gone away. Laura can eat only unadulterated, organic products—which are in short supply at the Safeway but are available en masse at Good Earth, the health food store located in Fairfax, the next town up. If Marin County is the crunchiness capital of the United States, and Fairfax is the epicenter of crunchiness in Marin, than it is fair to say that Good Earth is the crunchiest place in the U.S.A.

In the months ahead I will look forward to plying its aisles, exchanging hellos with uniformly friendly and helpful employees who lay waste to my preconceptions about this place. I have always found the store a bit frightening, you see. Dispatched there periodically by Laura to pick up, say, a salmon filet or mustard greens or extra-virgin olive oil, I've been intimidated by the profusion of zealous and seemingly mirthless vegans: stringy men with earrings and manes; braless women in peasant skirts; Wiccans and aging hippies who do not smile at my children. Driving past it once, I heard Willa say, from the backseat, "There goes the Grumpy People's Store."

"Why do you call it that?" I said.

"Mommy says the people in there are grumpy because they don't eat meat" came the reply.

"She says what they need is a steak and a martini," added Devin.

Before we leave for Good Earth, Laura and I take inventory in our kitchen. "As you can see, we're out of milk and low on bread," she says. I had not, while taking in the random jumble of fridge contents, leapt to those conclusions. But I nod as if I had.

We drive to Fairfax, find a spot next to a Datsun with an ENLIGHTEN UP bumper sticker, and my apprenticeship begins in earnest. Laura has brought her own reusable cloth grocery bags and her own recycled plastic bags, one of which she commences filling with blood oranges. "These just came in, and Devin loves them," she says. "Learn to shop seasonally—take advantage of what the season offers."

The beginning of blood orange season has coincided with the end of football season. It is Super Sunday. I am missing trenchant pregame analysis. I keep my mouth shut. Football is no longer my world.

I follow Laura around the store taking notes for the day I will make this lonely circuit on my own.

Think about vegetables. The kids will always eat broccoli and carrots . . . Everything you buy here, you should use within the week . . . Always get one head of lettuce and one winter green, although I'm not a big fan of spinach . . . These are mustard greens, this is rainbow chard, this is red chard, this is dinosaur kale . . . Always get a bunch of celery and a couple cucumbers. I need things to munch on.

There is a ponytailed guy doing some stocking over by the winter root vegetables. Laura tells me he is a conspiracy theorist.

Right now he is riffing on the president, saying, "He actually seems like a decent enough guy. I could see smoking a joint with him, but you definitely don't want him running the country."

We swing by the meat counter—the store's leading profit center, tolerated by vegans and vegetarians as a necessary evil—to stock up on flesh for the week. "I can eat the chicken sausage with sun-dried tomatoes and mushrooms," says Laura, "but not with apricots or apples. The fruit somehow interferes with my digestion of protein."

I nod as if to say, *Of course it does,* while thinking, *Sucks to be you.*

"And get hot dogs," says Laura. "The kids won't eat the fish."

Before sending me off in search of the special, organic Tacherra Ranch eggs recommended by her nutiritionist, Laura warns me, "Watch you don't get the Tacherra duck eggs by mistake."

The cart is nearly full as Laura ticks off the last three items on the list: "Tampons, toothpaste, and ginger."

I invite her to hunt down her own tampons or, as Devin calls them, "toupons."

She declines, pointing out, "If they're on the list, you're going to need to know where to find them. You might as well get used to it."

I locate the tampons. "They're not for me," I say at the counter as the checkout woman scans them. She is pallid and serious in appearance, with spiky, close-cropped hair and thick frames. To my surprise, she smiles, and I am encouraged.

BACK AT HOME, WITH THE CHILDREN LOOKING ON, LAURA announces, "Okay, this is a very important moment." With that, she hands me the red apron, which I solemnly don. Catching a glimpse of myself in the kitchen window, I notice how the apron frames my shoulders and sets off my pectorals to flattering effect.

"You look silly," says Willa.

"You're not used to seeing me in an apron," I counter. "But I think I'll grow into this job."

"I don't think you can."

I've been picking up on these low-level vibes of anxiety from Willa ever since Laura and I started talking about pulling a switcheroo. They are a measure of the intelligence of this special eight-year-old. She enjoys roughhousing and is not above indulging in, say, a midafternoon Creamsicle, if I'm buying, or the usually verboten weeknight access to Nickelodeon, if Mom is out at book group. But she's smart enough to know that promoting the corrupt cop to chief of police might not be a good thing for the city, or the household. It would be wrong to say she's withholding judgment on our imminent Experiment. She's already passed judgment on it. She's sure it's doomed.

"Why did you think I can't do this?" I ask her.

"You don't know how to cook."

"But I'm going to cook, starting tomorrow, most of our meals for the next six months."

"You're just like, not the mom. You don't know how to do it."

I can't argue with her. I can only try to pleasantly surprise her.

THAT NIGHT, WHEN ALL THE OTHERS HAVE GONE TO BED, I SURF over to A&E and find *Shackleton*—Kenneth Branagh as that early-twentieth-century British explorer, trying to save the lives of his crew after their ship, the *Endurance,* is crushed and devoured by pack ice in the Antarctic. I'd been riveted earlier in the week by the History Channel as it rehashed the particulars of Custer's Last Stand. Whose journey will mine more closely resemble? Am I the rash and vainglorious buffoon, leading my army down the Rosebud, about to plunge headlong into battle with an adversary much, much more formidable than I realize? Or will I, like Shackleton, take some serious lumps but ultimately and heroically avert catastrophe, and write a happy ending?

On the screen, Branagh has just given the order to shoot the dogs, whose meat will sustain them. "I cannot afford to be sentimental," he tells the men. "If I am, you will die—die frozen, die starving, die mad."

Tomorrow morning begins my own odyssey to parts unknown. My gaze falls upon the ironically named Spike, the effete and craven standard poodle curled at my feet. (Laura wanted a dog but is allergic to dog fur. So we ended up with a poodle who trembles at the sight of his own reflection in the mirror.) I ask myself, *How difficult would it be to sacrifice this effete beast, bouffant and all, if the humans in the family were starving?*

"Not very difficult," I inform Spike.

I find myself thinking what Shackleton's men must have found themselves thinking as the ice closed in around them: *What in the world have I gotten myself into?*

Play Ball!

So much for a smooth transition. We are awakened at 4:15 on Morning 1 by the low moans of Devin, whose face is covered with a sheen of perspiration.

That's not particularly noteworthy, in and of itself. We're talking about a seventy-five-pound six-year-old who pretty much sweats in his sleep every night. As I see it, he is all but assured of growing up to be one of those offensive linemen on the back of whose football pants appears a gigantic sweat crescent before the game is five minutes old. Someday, if he's good enough, John Madden will be circling D's blotch with his Telestrator stylus while declaiming, "That right there—that's something you don't see on a wide receiver!"

Devin perspires the way other children draw breath. His temperature this morning, however, is a legitimate concern. The expensive thermometer with the digital readout, the one you stick in their ears, says 102.3. I get some water and kiddie Tylenol into him and start changing my plans for the day.

After making Willa's breakfast and lunch, I drop her off at Brookside Elementary School, an uncomplicated-sounding task that is made unpleasantly tense by a parking circle that requires, for maximum efficiency, a small modicum of consideration and thoughtfulness on the part of the motorists using it.

Upon my return, Laura is reading the papers and finishing a leisurely breakfast. Willa's and my breakfast dishes, along with the detritus of the lunch I prepared, remain on the counter. How serious is she about letting me do everything? Very serious.

"I was going to call school to tell them Devin won't be in today," she said. "Then I remembered, that's *your* job." She gives me a peck on the cheek and, with a chipper "Good luck!," is out the door.

Her commute is reasonable. Our office is a converted garage behind the house. It is fifteen paces, door to door, although the psychological distance is far greater. For a refuge, it sits perilously close to our living quarters, but it is all we have, so we make it work for us. When the children have the audacity to come knocking, we explain to them that we are busy earning the money for food and gifts—Christmas and birthday—then banish them.

With Laura gone, it is just us guys, D and me, sharing some guy time. He's on the couch with a psychedelic Magical Mystery Tour bus for which I overpaid last summer at a Santa Monica hobby shop. Our kids like the Beatles.

"Is Ringo the one who looks like that guy in *The Princess Bride*?"

"Which guy?"

"The Spaniard."

"Yes, absolutely." Ringo and Mandy Patinkin have dark, unruly manes. I'll give him that one.

"Is this the bus the Beatles took to concerts?"

"I don't know. Probably. Actually, yes, I'm sure it was."

"If there were four of them, why were there so many seats?"

And so on.

Devin's interest in the Beatles transcends his delight in hearing "Ob-La-Di, Ob-La-Da." His morbid curiosity about the death of John Lennon—we told him the sad truth—is of a piece with his fascination with catastrophes on a grander scale. The bombing of Pearl Harbor and the sinking of the *Titanic* have been reenacted many times in our home and bathtub. While he will finish kindergarten not quite able to write every letter in the alphabet, he can give you the final casualty count from the *Titanic* (1,517 souls); can tell you how many of its watertight bulkheads were breached (five), and how many breached bulkheads it was designed to survive (four). Thanks to his Pearl Harbor flash cards—I picked them up on that Slater assignment—he knows the difference between a "Zero" fighter and a "Kate" torpedo bomber. He can rattle off the names of many of the ships moored at Battleship Row on that December morning, and has watched *Tora! Tora! Tora!* from beginning to end.

He's still running a mild fever, so I green-light some TV. Laura descends from her aerie within the hour to use the john and, on her way out, dispense a tip or two:

"A work-at-home mom with a sick child will take advantage of the time to get some housecleaning done."

I nod agreeably and keep doing what I've been doing—scrubbing potatoes for that night's dinner. "If I were you," she says, seeing the rock cod I've taken out to thaw, "I'd put that back in the freezer and use the salmon in the fridge. The salmon doesn't freeze as well as rock cod."

I hear and obey.

Laura is back among us at lunchtime, with Devin well into the *Harry Potter and the Sorcerer's Stone* video. Pointing to the piles of folded laundry that I'd hoped she would notice, she does not compliment me but, rather, lodges a minor complaint: "I like my socks folded together, not just lying next to each other. Otherwise you end up with a houseful of odd socks."

After lunch, she goes outside to get the mail. "This is for you," she says, handing me the San Anselmo '03 Recreation catalog. "Smart working moms"—by which Laura means, well, Laura— "get their kids signed up for camp early."

Yeah, well, it's early February, I think, and in case you haven't noticed, I'm rolling Her Majesty's socks into tidy bundles. As it happens, I don't get the kids signed up for Millennium Madness or Camp Rad that day. Or that week. Or that month, or the next one, or the next, or the next.

Laura will prove a font of excellent advice during these early weeks. Why do I allow so much of it to roll off my back? Part of the problem is the sheer volume. So free is she with tips and suggestions that I begin to feel ever so slightly hectored and overwhelmed.

While I take note of her suggestions—hell, I write most of them down—I do not take them to heart. I'm not ready for them, or worthy of them. I want praise. What I don't want, but am getting by the boatload, is advice and constructive criticism. I've said all the right things—*This is going to be the hardest thing I've ever done*—but secretly felt, deep in my heart, that I would master it quickly. It's *housework*. How tough could it be? I am guilty of hubris. I am in trouble.

———

THE SALMON IS FINE, THOUGH A BIT PLAIN, LAURA BEING ALLERGIC to any sauce that might have enlivened it. The kids' turkey dogs are a success, but then you really have to try to screw them up (turkey dogs, not kids). The potatoes are, in Devin's words, "an apostrophe."

I diced them, I mixed them with olive oil and sea salt in a glass bowl, I roasted them for an hour at 425. "Next time, try four hundred," says Laura upon examining the spuds, which look, at first glance, only moderately dessicated and overdone. Attempting to spatula them off the pan, however, I realize their undersides are hideously blackened. They are also badly over-salted, although the charring issue trumps that problem. Desperate to salvage the starch, I spend a quarter hour massaging each spud between thumb and forefinger, attempting to remove the carbon and excess salt. I then dim the dining room lights—ostensibly to create ambience, in reality to prevent the children from seeing the potatoes, which remain inedible despite my best efforts. Willa lifts one to within a half foot of her mouth before catching sight of its anthracite-colored underside. The look she casts me conveys less annoyance than pity.

"That's okay, Dad," she says. "You're just starting out. Could you make me some toast?"

AT DINNER THE FOLLOWING NIGHT DEVIN SURPRISES ME—AND secretly pleases his mother—by announcing, "Daddy wouldn't play with me today."

A bald-faced lie. Earlier that afternoon, we'd restored the LocoSound on his RailKing die-cast metal Southern Pacific

———

line. The kid was so thrilled to hear his train whistle again, I think he sprung a little Woodrow. But then I had to bail at four o'clock to get dinner going, so now I'm the male version of Miss Grundy.

Sensing blood in the water, Willa pounces as well: "He *used* to be a fun daddy. Now he doesn't play with us."

First of all, Willa, I noticed you had trouble enunciating that complaint because your mouth is full of dinner I cooked for you, which prevented me from playing after four P.M., it's true. Please, don't thank me. Your gratitude is understood.

Second of all, you're the one who is eight going on eighteen, who all of a sudden doesn't want to hold her father's hand in public, even when we're crossing streets, and who has posted a Keep Out sign on her bedroom door.

Not fun? *Moi?* Who picks you up—when you allow it—holds you parallel to the ground, the way King Kong held Fay Wray, then spins you onto the sofa? Who smuggles you flashlights so you can keep reading after lights-out? (I don't like to undercut Laura's authority, but I remember from my own Pennsylvania boyhood the bitter tyranny of the etched-in-stone lights-out, when all I needed was a few more minutes to finish a key chapter in, say, *The Tower Treasure* or *The Missing Chums*.)

While this minor uprising reveals their perfidy and ingratitude, it also attests to their powers of perception. Because even though I've been doing this job for just thirty-six hours, the dynamic has definitely changed. The way it's always broken down in our house, Laura wears the black hat, announcing the imminence of sunscreen application, baths, toothbrushing, bedtime. I'm more of a bread-and-circuses kind of emperor. I fly in from wherever I've been, dispense gifts and treats, and commence roughhousing. I have not been mindful of the Routine because if the Routine broke down just a bit, I wouldn't be around to suffer the consequences. I'd be in Collegeville or College Station or State College, poring over a room-service menu in the heartland.

Now I have a vested, selfish interest in preserving order, in keeping the trains running on time. Mr. Fun Guy, as the children once knew me, has a bit of Mussolini in him, it turns out. As interesting as the alacrity with which the kids have picked up on my new despotism is the pleasure Laura takes from hearing me criticized. Maybe I'm not such a congenial person after all. Maybe everyone is garrulous and carefree who doesn't have to prepare for a party of fifty—Laura's fortieth birthday is at our house Saturday night—and make ten meals a day.

My poll numbers with the children, usually higher than Laura's, have been artificially inflated by my avoidance of many of the unpleasant duties of parenting. Now Laura looks on with pleasure while those numbers head south.

Devin returns to school Tuesday, Willa is out sick Wednesday, I owe *SI* a column on Thursday—the same day I volunteer to help in my daughter's class garden, where we harvest lettuce leaves, and Catherine O. asks me if I wouldn't mind removing the dog turds that have somehow ended up around one of the planters. While I discharge that duty, a very bright boy named Stephen S. gives me a brief talk on the black widow:

"If you're bitten by a black widow, it helps if you're middle-aged. If you're in your seventies, you have a better chance of dying than living. If you're a baby, forget it.

"That's why you want to clean out your garage and get all the traps ready. In my house, there was a black widow, but my mother smashed it with a hammer, then drilled its head with the electric drill."

I make a mental note to give Stephen's mother a slightly wider berth in the future.

On Friday, while cutting an onion for the roast chicken, I slice the tip of my right index finger, bandage it up, and get back in the kitchen, back in the game. That is the night the spaghetti squash refuses to cook. Three times I remove it from the oven, three times it has to go back. Proud though I am of the lettuce-radicchio-avocado salad I've prepared, there isn't enough of it to go around. Laura's father, Robert, has been invited to dinner, it turns out.

"No one told me," I protest, sotto voce, in the kitchen.

"It's the chef's job to ask," says Laura, handing the blame right back to me.

That night I am comatose in the bath, holding my sliced finger up to soothe the throbbing, when Laura comes in and sits down. She inquires as to whether I've had a chance to sign the kids up for any camps. She wonders if I've arranged to have Spike boarded for the weekend we'll be away in April. She wants to know if I've lined up any babysitters for our date night.

"Laura," I say, "if you're going spend six months badgering me about things I've done wrong or haven't done but need to do, we're not going to need a babysitter for date night, if you catch my drift."

"I'm just trying to help," she says, stiffening. "I assume you want to do the job properly."

"I do." But I need the carrot, once in a while. "I'm busting my ass here, and I need some acknowledgment of that."

She smiles. "It's hard, isn't it?"

After she leaves, and I've had the chance to marinate a while longer in self-pity, I realize that I'm feeling sorry for the wrong person. I've signed up for a half year of this; Laura has already been doing it for nine, and will be re-upping, come August, for another decade or so.

It's hard, isn't it? It's not hard. It's friggin' impossible. I'm trying to make deadlines while cooking and cleaning and volunteering and entertaining. Is it this hard all the time? Can she possibly have been enduring this for nine years, while I floated alongside in ignorant bliss? Maybe I should have spent a little more on her birthday present.

I AM PROUD OF THE SHINDIG WE THROW FOR LAURA. I RENT glasses, plates, silver, and a couple of big heat lamps for the deck. I order, then pick up, a small fortune's worth of food from a local restaurant called Insalata's. Twenty minutes before the gig kicks off, my mother-in-law, Josephine, arrives. I'm not saying Josi had low expectations for the Experiment, but as soon as she heard about it, she offered to arrange for prayers to be said on my behalf at the Silent Unity Prayer Vigil Chapel in Missouri.

I am thanking her for that kind offer when she says, looking around, "Aus, where's the food?"

I call her attention to the dozen or so large foil containers stacked on the kitchen counter.

"Is it put together?" she asks.

"It comes put together!" I reply, pointing to the place on the take-out menu where it says, *Pick them up and entertain effortlessly!*

Apparently, I've interpreted that passage too literally. Softly taking the Savior's name in vain, Josi springs into action. She locates, then dusts off several platters on which to lay out the goat cheese crostini with chanterelle mushrooms. She assembles, then dresses the Caesar salad. She removes the marinated olives and bay leaves from their containers; the piquillo peppers stuffed with goat cheese from theirs; then artfully arranges everything on an enormous tray I've forgotten we own. She is just about finished when company starts showing up. Nice work, Jos. I'll know better next time.

My toast, which has basically written itself, begins with a salute to our guests for having the courage to travel in spite of the terror alert level, which had been elevated to orange the day before. I then allow as how my attempt to handle everything Laura has handled for close to a decade has left me many things: "frustrated, bleeding, on tiptoe to disable the smoke alarm; not in the mood tonight, dear.

"Mostly it has left me with a dramatically deepened appreciation for everything Laura has done for us: running a household, paying bills, doing taxes, shopping—all the while carving out a few hours a week to conduct interviews, write magazine stories and revise the screenplay that will eventually be our ticket out of this gingerbread starter house.

"Because of fate, my travel—and, let's face it, my selfishness and sloth—Laura has shouldered more than her share of the hard work of our marriage; has been, frankly, the only authentic adult in the house. Fairly or unfairly, it has fallen to her to handle the duties I'm just now discovering, from what will go into the children's stomachs to what will go into their heads; from nutrition to religion. She ponders that stuff while I ponder the route I'll take on the mountain bike that day: Eldridge to the top of Tam, or maybe the Pine Mountain loop?"

I wrap it up with some cheap reference to how hot she looks

at forties, and raise my glass. "To my soul mate and role model, my chief of Homeland Security, the love of my life."

Rereading the toast months later, I will see a paean to a beautiful, strong, intelligent woman. I will also want to shout at the author—that would be me—"Okay, well, maybe it's time for you to get your ass in gear, time to start pulling your load. It's time for you to grow up!"

Cupid, Kiss My Ass

Please do not think me unromantic or a misanthrope when I confess that Valentine's Day, today, is about as welcome to me as the sight of an unidentified hair in a hotel bathtub.

It comes at a bad time. I've got Christmas, then I've got Laura's birthday, followed a scant eleven days later by Valentine's. It's too many command performances, gift- and card-wise, in a tight space—too many opportunities to blow it.

A few years ago I got smart and covered my butt, investing $13.95 for a box of ten cards. The cards feature a series of black-and-white photographs by Robert Doisneau. In one, a guy is mashing face with his date in a movie theater. In another, a guy in a muscle shirt is pressing himself into a woman whose gown has fallen well down her shoulder. There, in the next, is a woman in a convertible, lying across the lap of her date, who has slid over to the non–steering wheel side—this is Parking Strategies and Techniques 101—to give her greater range of movement.

Every Valentine's morning for the last four years I've pulled this box of cards out of my file cabinet, grabbed one, then taken seven or so minutes to compose something that passes, hopefully, for heartfelt. I've sealed the envelope, propped it against a candlestick on the dining room table, and considered myself done. I don't feel bad giving this holiday short shrift. The truth is, I'm still living off the fat of my Valentine's present to Laura a few years ago, when I underwent a certain twenty-minute elective procedure. I bring it up now to let readers know that, even before our little role reversal, I knew a little something about being emasculated. As Laura had pointed out when we were in negotiations, "This would be one of the most generous things you could ever do for me."

It would also give me an excuse to phone it in on Valentine's Day—which fell the day after I underwent the Big Snip. I planned to give her one of the cards. For the balance of your Valentine's gift, I would say if I detected any sulking, *any petulance whatsoever,* please see my recently ventilated scrotum.

In addition to some garden-variety Snip-related concerns— What if I want more kids later? How much is this going to hurt? How soon will I be back on my bike?—I was nagged, as the moment of truth approached, by the notion that I was about to become a party to an act of betrayal against myself. Thirty-eight years of meritorious service, My Boys would have been within their rights to complain, and this is the thanks we get. I was Judas; I was the McMurtry protagonist forced by the caprices of the llano to shoot his trusty steed. Good-bye, Old Paint, indeed.

On the big day, I was summoned from the waiting room by Nurse Ratched's less charismatic younger sister, who informed me, as we walked to the clean, well-lighted OR where my cojones would be transformed into harmless show balls, "You are scheduled to undergo a vazzectomy"—that's how the pros pronounce it. "You realize this procedure will render you sterile." She paused for emphasis. "Unable to have children." *Last exit before bridge.*

When you're about to get your vasectomy and the nurse says that to you, do me a favor and reply, "But I was told it would clear my sinuses." What I actually mumbled was "That's the idea, pretty much."

She told me to strip and handed me a robe. She said I could leave my socks on. I removed them.

Enter the urologist, wearing a shower cap and spouting false cheer. He told me to lie down and, without so much as a by-your-leave, flipped my robe up to my sternum and commenced with the dry shave, briskly defoliating the area while complaining about CBS's coverage of the Nagano games.

Next came a series of cold unguents, followed by the injection of a local anesthetic, followed by the death of virility.

While the urologist and nurse merrily went about their incising and severing and cauterizing, I mentioned, with poorly feigned nonchalance, that my neighbor's diabetic brother-in-law had suffered postvasectomy complications that had left him with a withered testicle, which put me in mind of a limerick I'd once read in a James Herriott novel:

> *There once was a man from Devises*
> *Whose balls were of different sizes.*
> *The one was so small*

41

It was no ball at all,
But the other won several prizes.

Before I could finish, the urologist was nodding—he'd heard it before. Of course he had. He was a urologist. It turned out that the nurse was a Herriott fan; she had, in fact, once met the author on a trip to England. Thus did I find myself congratulating her, as she helped neuter me, on her signed copy of *All Creatures Great and Small.* That's when the urologist grazed some unanesthetized nerve bundle, causing me to flop like a flounder on the deck of a Boston Whaler.

"I'll stay out of that area" was all the good doctor said, once I'd fallen silent. As I told him how I sure would appreciate it, it occurred to me what a piss-poor spy or martyr I would have made.

Dressing, I regretted having worn jeans to the hospital, but not as much as I regretted having removed my socks. (Think about it. You've just had your wedding tackle sliced and diced. Your anesthetic is wearing off. Ever so gingerly, you don a snug pair of jeans, thinking all the while: If I had this to over again, I'd wear something more loose fitting. Now, because you forgot to do it earlier, you must lean over—the jeans are rearranging things Down There, straining stitches—and pull on a pair of socks.)

For the rest of the day I felt like I'd been kicked in the groin. By Sunday I was mincing around the house but still allowing Laura to bring me food. "You make an excellent serving wench," I joked that afternoon, hoisting a tuna sandwich:

"You make an excellent eunuch," she riposted.

Fifty hours: that's how long my grace period lasted. Before you surrender your live ammo, your partner will tell you what a profound demonstration of your love it will be. For fifty or so hours afterward, if you're lucky, she will spare you the eunuch jokes. It was Laura, post–grace period, who coined the term "show balls"; Laura who noted, feigning surprise, that my voice had not ascended. My forfeiture of virility resulted not so much in a loss of masculinity as in a loss of dignity.

Just something to gird for, guys, if you're thinking about getting snipped. Remember to milk those fifty hours, should you decide to go through with it. And leave your socks on.

IT IS ONLY IN A FIGURATIVE SENSE, THIS PARTICULAR VALENTINE'S day, that I have given blood. On this, Morning 11 of my new life, Laura embarks on a four-day trip to Catalina. She is reporting a travel piece for *VIA* magazine. While packing, she is full of hollow assurances that she will miss us, but I notice a serious spring in her step as she walks out the door. If she had the hops to pull it off, I think she might have leapt in the air and clicked her heels together.

Even with Alie, our occasional babysitter, giving me five hours on Thursday and Friday (noon to five), the late afternoons are intense. I've got school pickups, grocery shopping (when you're new at this, you forget items and have to double back repeatedly). There is homework enforcement and, if I'm on the ball, the preparing of tomorrow's lunches while cooking tonight's dinner. Evenings drag on, as I rush to get the kitchen clean before marshaling my strength for the Final Push, the Last Ordeal, the get-'em-in-jammies, read-'em-a-book, brush-their-teeth, lights-out quadrathlon.

As will remain the pattern throughout the Experiment, mornings will provide the stage for our worst behaviour. Mornings are

when Willa and Devin force me to ask the deepest, most profound questions of myself:

If I love these children, which I do, unconditionally, why is
that right now I *really* don't like them?

Are there listings for "exorcist" in the yellow pages?

What sort of flawed adult can be reduced to trembling, impo-
tent fury by an eight-year-old and her little brother?

Who taught Devin the word *asshole*?

It is unfair of me to include Willa in all these rants, for she
is merely huffy, insolent, and sporadically disobedient, as
opposed to the aggressive malevolence of her brother, who lies
every morning like a slug on the sofa until 7:53 or so, knowing
that we need to be out of the house by eight o'clock.

On our first morning *sans* Mommy, after asking him for the
seventh time to put his socks on, I up the ante with a bit of
profanity: "Put your goddam socks on, we're already five minutes late!"

That lapse is his cue to reach into his own expanding arsenal
of adult language. This week's forbidden word: *asshole*. When I
let cross my lips the phrase "goddam socks" he looks up from
the RailKing catalog and asks, "Why are you being such an asshole?" Except that, because of the retainer he began wearing
two weeks ago to counter his severe underbite, it comes out:

"Why are you being thuch an athhole?"

I deserve that. I have set a poor example. It was a good bust.
But my feelings are hurt the following morning, when I remain
preternaturally calm while trying to lure Willa to the bathroom,
where we need to fashion her pigtails.

"If we get a late start today," I scold as she refuses to lift her
head from *Captain Underpants and the Wrath of the Wicked
Wedgie Woman,* "I don't want to hear you complaining to

Mommy about it." (She'd tattled on me the night before.) "If we're late, you'll know why."

From the kitchen comes the voice of a six-year-old convinced he is sticking up for his sister:

" 'Cauth you're an athhole?"

"THAT'S FIFTEEN MINUTES OFF HIS BEDTIME, RIGHT THERE, NO IFS, ands, or buts. And you have to follow through on the punishment."

I am on the phone with Laura, who on the third night of her trip has just checked into a $450 room in Catalina. She wants to talk to the children, but this poses a problem. If I walk into the living room with the phone, she will hear Squidward and SpongeBob going at it in the background and know that her no-TV-during-the-week rule is being flouted. (I never begin a day intending to cave on the no-TV policy, but the tube's behavior-modification powers sometimes prove irresistible.) Leaving the phone in the bedroom, I summon the children individually. The first thing Devin blurts is "Daddy let us watch the end of *Harry Potter*."

Even though this is true—it made our first evening go that much more smoothly—I fix Devin with the stinkeye while slashing my index finger across my throat. "Actually," he blurts, "I was lying. We didn't watch *Harry Potter*."

I can only wince at this shoddy and amateurish piece of dissembling. *Jesus, kid,* I feel like saying, *if you can't lie better than that, don't bother.*

I know I am deeply in the wrong here, that the children must be taught the importance of telling the truth. On the other hand, the lad did have my back when he told the fib.

Laura isn't buying his recantation and tells me, quietly but firmly, "I will not allow the quality of their lives to be affected by your experiment."

Little late for that. I mean, when did they get to bed last night? Eleven sharp? We got a late start on dinner, and things snowballed from there.

I pose a hypothetical question to Laura: "If you forgot—and I'm not saying I have—to take the ground beef out of the freezer earlier, how might you thaw it in time for dinner?"

"I could microwave it," says Laura, "but then it would cook unevenly. Good thing you didn't forget to take it out of the freezer. You know we're out of sauce," she continues, correctly guessing that I intend to make spaghetti.

"That's all right," I say, exhaling, "because I forgot to thaw the ground beef."

What rankles is that Laura had accompanied me to Good Earth for my last expedition for groceries. Knowing we needed sauce, she remained silent as I wheeled the cart past jar upon jar of the stuff.

"I was there in case you had questions," she explains now with perverse amusement. "You're not going to learn unless you make mistakes."

I make the mistake of telling her about a call earlier in the day from my friend and adventure-racing teammate Gordon Wright. He wasn't going into the office and wondered if I wanted to join him in some kayaking.

It was a poor idea on many fronts. I owed a story to *SI for Kids,* and I needed to pay some bills. I asked Gordon how soon he could pick me up.

We zipped down to Sausalito and rented a two-person kayak from a woman named Cheyenne. She was in her mid-twenties, tanned, and toned. I was filling out my form, chatting her up. I may have mentioned some of the kayaking I'd done in some of the adventure races in which Gordon and I have competed. I didn't tell her about our blooper reel on the Kern River a couple of years ago, when we spent more time out of the boat than in it. Cheyenne seemed to be into my rap until Gordon sabotaged it with malice aforethought. "We'll be back in less than two hours," he said, "because Mr. Mom here has to pick up his kids."

The G-Man and I were soon gliding past yachts and dread-noughts, then, after fifteen minutes, looking up at the multimillion-dollar Tiburon mansions built into the cliffs above us. Squadrons of cormorants swooped toward us, then sheared off on either side. Harbor seals surfaced nearby. We crossed Raccoon Strait, then paddled along the coast of Angel Island. A flood tide made the return trip more arduous, and that was okay. As Gordon had told Cheyenne, I had to pick the kids up at school. If I had to walk through the parking lot, better to do it in a sweat-dampened T-shirt.

As I relate this midafternoon outing to my wife, she seems incredulous.

"Are you kidding?"

"Believe me," I say, "it wasn't that impressive. We didn't go that far."

"Believe me," she replies, "I'm not impressed." She explains that what I've done is unthinkable. "Every minute of your day is accounted for. You've got to make lists, and then attack the list. You've got to be ruthlessly efficient. You get the kids to school, you've got a block of time in the office, you take advantage of it. If you don't comprehend that, you're screwed before you start."

Sobered by her rebuke, I attack Tuesday with a plan. I will tidy for an hour, then get some wash going. I will put in two solid hours in the office, then maybe squeeze a run in.

It is a plan with foresight, a solid plan, a plan that is derailed by C-SPAN2. While picking up toys in the living room, I find myself drawn into the drama of the confirmation hearing of Miguel Estrada, a candidate for the U.S. Court of Appeals. A cavalcade of senators appear on the screen: the avuncular Richard Durbin (D-Ill.), the recently disgraced and demoted Trent Lott (R-Miss.), the silver-haired, silver-tongued Chris Dodd (D-Conn.) Things aren't looking so hot for Estrada, which makes Judiciary Committee chairman Orrin Hatch (R-Utah) look even more dyspeptic than usual.

When the Senate breaks for lunch, the network cuts immediately to a White House briefing. I'm already an hour behind schedule—might as well make a pot of coffee and see what Ari Fleischer has to say. I admire his tie today: a burnished gold overlaid with a tasteful pattern. For a doctrinaire conservative he ties a rakish knot—rather long and narrow, canted slightly to the right—beneath which bloom a pair of pronounced dimples in the fabric. I love that, but I can never get my tie to do it. A line of questions concerning a new audiotape from Osama bin Laden elicits from the balding press secretary a mention of his concern "about the ties between Al Qaeda and Iraq," which leads to a discussion of the terror alert level.

At the same time it jacked us up to orange, the Department of Homeland Security also urged Americans to stock up on duct tape and plastic sheeting, in case of chemical or biological attack. We've got quite a few rolls of duct tape lying around. As for plastic sheeting, I'll use tarps, should agents of Al Qaeda hijack a crop-dusting plane and cover our fair town with a fine mist of, say, Sarin or some other deadly nerve agent. I know people who discount the possibility of that happening. Are they unfamiliar with the Homeland Security Advisory System? Aren't they listening? We're talking orange (high risk of terrorist attack) here! Not blue (general risk), not green (low risk). Orange.

Assuming these unfamiliar duties is taxing enough. Assuming them now, during this perilous stage in American history, makes the job that much tougher. In addition to Laura's twenty-three-point memo, I've got Dubya's latest Homeland Security Presidential Directive, dated February 7 and entitled, somewhat ominously, "Are You Ready?" It runs to eleven pages, the first of which contains this profundity:

Wherever you are, be aware of your surroundings. The very nature of terrorism suggests there may be little or no warning.

Other useful tips from the memo:

Know the location and availability of hard hats in buildings in which you spend a lot of time.

Learn first aid.

Be wary of packages or letters [with] handwritten or poorly typed addresses.

If you are trapped in debris . . . do not light a match.

In case of nuclear or radiological attack, do not look at the flash or fireball.

To save critical time during an emergency, *"sheeting should be premeasured and cut for each opening."*

Good call, Mr. Ridge. I'll bust out my tape measure and scissors and get right on that. As soon as I get back from my run.

Homemade Mayo

The baying of our cowardly poodle foretells the arrival at the front door of the Maguire kids—Robbie, Annie, and Maggie. I'm on carpool duty. We pile into the station wagon, the kids ganging up on me until I agree to take "the Hill Way"—a back-roads "shortcut" that entails ascending, then abruptly descending a 250-foot eminence. I take two lefts and a right and there he is, my man Albert, pulling up to the stop sign in that old maroon Beamer and damning his luck. He despises being stuck behind me; I never go more than fifteen miles per hour over the speed limit.

Don't get me wrong, I like Albert—pronounced Al-*bare*—a genuine Frenchman who owns a great little bistro in town. He greets me like a brother when I walk into the place; I don't think he realizes that I'm the guy whose ass he tailgates all the way to upper campus twice a week, on average.

Everybody needs to take a few deep, cleansing breaths and slow down in the morning. In the last few years we've had several pedestrians struck while trying to cross Sir Francis Drake Boulevard, which during the morning rush becomes, basically, a four-lane highway through the neighborhood. Just because it's the 'burbs doesn't mean there isn't danger around the next manicured corner. Take it from me: I was at lower campus the day the laughter turned to screams, the Octoberfest Saturday morning when the Astro Jump "bouncy" depressurized without warning.

One moment you're standing in line with your six-year-old son, waiting for his turn to climb in. The next moment the generator craps out and the fifteen-foot bouncy starts drooping like an octogenarian's erection, the walls and floor and ceiling all hemorrhaging air at once, the kids scrambling for the exit as their parents commence braying through the nylon mesh such helpful instructions as "Jimmy get out! GET OUT NOW!"

I joined a brigade of dads holding up the ceiling while Nancy S. crawled toward a pigtailed four-year-old who was too scared to move. "It's okay, honey. Come to me," she said, one arm outstretched. The child was too young to grasp that Nancy is one of the district's most formidable Power Mommies: ex–room parent, chairman of the Octoberfest Food Committee, year-round clearinghouse for gossip—a woman, in short, to be wordlessly, instantly obeyed.

But the little girl wouldn't budge. Her mother arrived during this impasse, elbowing Nancy aside and hurling her dumpling-like body across the bouncy's floor, now the consistency of a leaky waterbed, grabbing her daughter and pulling her out by the ankles, like a midwife performing a breech birth.

"That was very close," said one woman, when all the kiddies had been liberated. (It wasn't.)

"It could've been very serious," agreed another, the subtext of their remarks being, *And it would have been, if we weren't so quick thinking and valorous.*

The next and most important job, once the children were extricated, was, of course, to assign blame. The man from Astro Jump had assured us there was a four-hour supply of gas in the generator; it had run out after ninety minutes. Plus, he was swarthy and had an uncertain grasp of English. He wasn't one of us. He was going down.

I was inclined to cut the Astro Jump dude some slack. Which is another reason why I may never fit in with some of these Brookside moms, some of whom are possessed of an extraordinary sense of entitlement, particularly when it comes to their children's schools and anything to do with them.

"Is there any way," one mom had asked at a meeting of the school's Site Council earlier that week, "we could put up, like, an enormous protective shade or awning, to keep the sun off the children during recess?" A more sensible parent suggested, "Perhaps your child could just wear a hat."

While they can be meddlesome and occasionally delusional, these are the same women who deserve most of the credit for making Brookside what it is: a little citadel of excellence, an example of what can be accomplished with public education when mediocrity is not an option.

Although it may lack a supersized sunshade over the playground, Brookside features after-school enrichment programs in art, music, poetry, photography, French, and Spanish. At an age when my primary after-school activities consisted of learning to smoke and shoplift, my nine-year-old daughter will be learning to play the flute *and* conjugating the verb *être*. These programs are bankrolled by a parent-run foundation. Brookside gets an additional shot in the arm from Octoberfest, the very shindig that had brought Devin and me to school the morning of Bouncygate. So it was a bit lame, I thought, once the generator was back up and running, when a small queue of parents formed outside the Astro Jump. "Our son was inside when it collapsed," said the first guy in line. "We think we're entitled to a refund."

You are, sir, I thought, just as we are entitled to mock you behind your back for being a caviling weenie. Here are your three fifty-cent tickets back. Better luck in the Haunted House. Putz.

More important than Brookside's enrichment programs are the educators in its classrooms. Every teacher either of our children has had at this terrific little school has made us want to drop to our knees and thank the Lord. In the lottery of kindergarten teachers, Devin has drawn the wise, whimsical, wonderful, and (almost) infinitely patient Jan Bishop, in whose classroom I volunteer on Mondays. Even though Thursday, February 13, would be the hundredth day of school, Jan announced a week or so ahead of time that she would be absent that day. In her stead arrived a special substitute: Jan's hundred-year-old grandmother. On the special day, the children were greeted—somewhat cantankerously—by a white-haired cane-wielding centenarian who nonetheless bore a powerful resemblance to her granddaughter Jan. At 12:30, when Jan came clean to the class, blowing her own cover, there arose from the kindergartners a collective "I *knew* it!"

In her online, state-of-the-art weekly bulletin, Jan listed some of the clues the kids had picked up on, the details that had tipped the little gumshoes off to her true identity:

1. My voice sounded the same (I changed it slightly).
2. My rings were the same.
3. My teeth were the same.
4. I knew all their names before they told them to me.

I'd dropped in at the classroom to see her getup myself. I'd left more impressed with Jan than ever—I love her blithe, who-cares-what-other-people-think? lack of self-consciousness—but also wondering about myself. What sort of guy looks at a woman who is dressed up to resemble her grandmother and thinks, *You know, she looks kind of hot.*

Willa has been equally blessed, having been assigned to the third-grade classroom of the preternaturally organized Ruth Leader, whose kindness and warm smile mask a steely determination to wring as much as is humanly possible from each of her students. Make no mistake, the woman has her quirks. There she was on Back-to-School Night, September 4, standing before us in a turtleneck, even though it was eighty-five degrees in the room. As I would later find out, Ruth had good reason to keep her neck covered—she'd recently had tissue carved out of it. Ten days earlier, she'd had a biopsy. The day before she stood in front of us in that turtleneck, talking about math centers and Miwok Indians, the biopsy had come back. Ruth had cancer.

It turned out she had non-Hodgkin's lymphoma, a slow-growing cancer that was nonetheless widespread in her body, ruling out radiation as a treatment option. She would undergo chemotherapy. She set up a treatment regimen that would allow her, incredibly, to keep teaching. That blew me away.

The strange part, if you ask me, is that even though Ruth is getting treatments one week a month, on Tuesday, Wednesday, and Thursday, she looks good. She has a kind of glow. The chemo cleared up her dry skin, she tells me. Her beautician insisted that Ruth's hair became thicker during her treatments. Ruth confesses to me that people who haven't seen her in a while have been remarking, "Gee, you look great!"

We are having this chat at the Valentine's party in the multipurpose room. Gloria B., our room parent nonpareil—whose most recent triumph was guiding the children through the cutting, pressing, and sewing of a class quilt, for Christ's sake—is supervising the preparation of strawberry shortcake. The woman is so good, so in charge, as she says things like "I need a sifter!" and "Okay, who has the baking soda?" that it is difficult not to default into spectator mode and chat with the other moms.

Leaving the party, I swing by the office to check out the artwork on the wall. February has been dubbed Empathy and Tolerance Month at Brookside. Third graders have contributed brief essays, accompanied by pictures, citing examples of those virtues. Willa's best friend, Kailey, has penned a modest ode to her wheelchair-bound uncle, which, though not exactly oozing empathy, is honest:

"Although I am not in a wheelchair my uncle is. I can imagine how it feels to sit around all day. Once my cousin and I helped him wash his van." She brings it home with this spasm of candor: "I never really see him much."

"I don't know what it feels like to be poor," writes Stephen S., my buddy the arachnid expert, speaking for many of his peers in this affluent county. "But I want to help the poor. I hope less people are poor in the future."

"Even though I am not blind," Cole H. writes, "I can imagine what it must feel like. My grandma is half blind, so I help her." It's very decent of you, Cole. Some kids might rearrange the furniture.

I see plenty of "empathies" but only one "tolerance." It is by Willa, who shares this: "My mom can't eat a lot of food. So when my family wants to go out, we have to ask my mom where she wants to go."

Left unstated is the obvious—to Willa, at any rate—that this is a major pain in the ass, but we *tolerate* it, because we love Mom, and if we didn't tolerate it, she might up and say, *Fine, the hell with it, you three can shop and cook for yourselves and pay the bills and run the house.*

Much easier to simply tolerate Mommy's . . . intolerances.

In the illustration, a young woman—the Willa figure—reads from a list that has unscrolled all the way to her feet. It is a list of restaurants. "This one?" asks Willa.

The Laura figure, shapely and blond in a pea-green dress, says, "Nope!"

LAURA WALKS INTO THE HOUSE EARLY THE NEXT EVENING AND WE race to hug her. "Oh my god," she says, "that smells so wonderful."

"It's just the potatoes," I tell her. "I was waiting until you got home to do the fish." It is so nice to hear a compliment that any resentment I may have been storing evanesces during our embrace.

"You know what I'm going to do to spice up our evening?" she says, looking saucily at me. Forty years old, I think, and she's still a minx.

"I'm going to make homemade mayonnaise. We need olive oil, egg yolks, lemon juice, and a little dry mustard. Murph, check the fridge and see if we've got some dill."

Idiots Like Me

Every week I induct a new member or two into a kind of Skull and Boneheads Society, a fraternity so top secret that its members have no idea they're in it.

It is the Unclear on the Concept Club. How do you get in? You betray your cluelessness to me. You let slip some remark along the lines of what Zach M. told me at Laura's fortieth, having learned we intended to change jobs. "You know what you need to do? You need to take this time to really sharpen up your golf game."

Like all the men who would follow him into the UCC, Zach could not wrap his mind around the idea that, if it wouldn't be plausible for a working mother in charge of housekeeping, carpooling, meals, laundry, bills, and more to casually announce to her family on Saturday morning, "Okay everybody, I'm gonna disappear for five hours—six if the girls and I decide to go for a few pops afterward!"—then it won't work for me, either.

For a while, until he gained clarity and located a clue, my buddy Gordon was a member, calling several times a week to tempt me with sequels to the Kayaking Scandal: "How about a couple hours on the climbing wall?" . . . "You know, it's been a long time since we've ridden Tamarancho—*too* long."

On a day he knew that dinner was my responsibility, my friend Neil announced, "I've taken the liberty of reserving a three-thirty tee time. Is that something you'd be interested in?" (I'm noticing an emerging pattern here—a subset created by the intersection of two sets: men who are unclear on the concept and men who golf.) Rex, my father, a member of not one but two excellent golf clubs, was rubber-stamped by the club's New Members Committee for his *très, très* droll phone messages that invariably began "I suppose you're in the kitchen baking cookies."

Adjacent to Rex's locker in the UCC clubhouse is the stall I have assigned Laura's father, Robert, who owes his membership to his too funny habit of asking, when he calls and I pick up, "Is this the lady of the house?" While we're at it, let's host a mass induction for pretty much every guy of that generation— all the men who don't know enough not to boast about the fact that they had five kids "but never changed a diaper!," who feel a flash of annoyance when there is little or no milk in the refrigerator, the better to wash down their Oreos during *SportsCenter,* but to whom it might never occur to purchase milk themselves.

I'm not judging the membership. They're not bad people. They're simply incomplete. I was unclear and incomplete myself. In preparation for my journey in Laura's shoes, I actually drafted a TRS (Testosterone Reclamation Strategy), for those days when I missed doing, you know, guy things—joining Gordo on one of those monster rides, or talking with Oklahoma defensive coordinator Mike Stoops about how the Sooners were going to shut Texas down. Read it and weep:

"I could join the local rugby club," I wrote, "lace up the old boots for the first time in ten years and take out my frustration on some effete winger trying to get around my end. On second thought, I'm forty-one. That effete winger would juke me into the pitch on his way to scoring."

Funny, I never make it over to rugby practice, and it isn't just because the kids might object to not eating on those nights. By early evening, when it would be time to practice, *I am tired.*

I'm not talking a just-ran-eight-miles or biked-thirty-five-miles kind of tired. This is a less specific, more profound weariness felt in the marrow of one's bones—the dazed, near-collapse feeling that attends, say, Hour 3 of following one's wife through department stores.

I thought I knew from exhaustion. I've pulled hundreds of all-nighters to make deadlines for *SI;* gone weekends without sleep during adventure races—Eco-Challenge-type events that Gordon and I do when we can get a hall pass from our spouses. None of those ordeals has matched the sustained, profound weariness I feel as Laura's replacement, sinking down at nine P.M., a marathon of work behind me, only to realize that I am sitting on compressed laundry, the folding of which leads me to despair. This is how one's identity slowly ebbs away, in the gulag of these thankless, mindless tasks.

Core-deep fatigue makes me more jealous of my sleep than I've ever been, and has resulted in at least one unusual coping strategy. More and more, I find myself sitting down to take a whiz. You may see that as a symptom of emasculation. I see it as a way to get off my feet for a few extra minutes every day.

"I don't see a problem with that," says Gordon, to whom I confide this strange and slightly alarming development. "As long as you don't find yourself putting a little potpourri on the back of the toilet tank. Then it would be time to worry."

My day job, the job to which I will return, is hard: fly somewhere, hustle for interviews with guys who aren't necessarily happy to talk to you, fly somewhere else, hustle for more interviews, go to the game, hustle for backstory on the guys you didn't talk to, stay up most or all of the night composing—what?— some stew of words from which, with luck, your editor will be able to extrapolate or extract some semblance of a magazine story. You hit the "send" button and, lo, a catharsis! *You're done!* For the next few hours, at any rate, the story is someone else's problem. You drive to the airport—in Oklahoma City or College Station or Eugene—with your finger on the "seek" button, casting about for just one great song to drown out the angst of whether or not the editors are going to like it.

Finally, the deadline-conquering hero arrives at home, there to sprawl diagonally across the sofa with several sections of the newspaper; there to gaze fondly at his spouse, who, strangely, does not always return his smile, or join him on the sofa— indeed, who does not ever seem to be off her feet.

But whose fault is that? the man thinks to himself. Maybe if she'd been a better steward of her time in my absence, she would be finished with her work, just as I am finished with mine. Why should I feel bad about reaping my just reward—leisure— simply because she has not managed her time as wisely as I have?

Because, moron, to her, the work you do *is* leisure. Before she can go out to the office and start in on paid work, Laura has to put in a half day of unpaid work to which there is no end. All those semihostile vibes I thought I might have been picking up from Laura before my Awakening, before the scales fell from my eyes—those weren't my imagination. She was, if not a simmering cauldron of resentment and bitterness, at least a teapot. I thought I'd earned the right to sit my ass down on the couch, but if I saw my old self now, I'd glower at me, too.

IT IS THE ENDLESSNESS OF THE JOB THAT FUELS THE RESENTMENT. And lately, I am one angry white male. I wore my cranky pants pretty much throughout Laura's week in Catalina—was periodically, as accused, an "athhole"—and don them again almost daily during the week that follows. Not coincidentally, there is no school that week. On the calendar, it says "President's Week," but, in a broad hint at median incomes in the district, everyone around here calls it "Ski Week."

Don't assume I suck at skiing just because I tell you that I have always found Ski Week—and skiing—overrated. When I was growing up in a suburb of Pittsburgh, the nuns at St. Joe's Elementary might've given us a week off in February, but you can bet no one called it Ski Week. To my mother, who, during the 1972–73 school year had a child at St. Joe's in every grade but fourth, it was God Give Me the Strength to Get Through These Next Five Days Week. For us, it could have been Lying in Wait Behind the Bradburns' Hedges to Pelt Cars with Snowballs Week or Thumbing to the Fox Chapel Plaza to Avail Ourselves of the Five-Finger Discount Week.

Here in Marin County, it's Ski Week. While the pull of the

Sierra Nevadas, three and a half hours east, is strong, it is trifling compared to the powerful social forces, the peer pressure to participate in the most financially ruinous activity this side of polo. Laura has made plans for us visit her mother and stepfather. Josi and Al live in a gorgeous and gleaming Tahoe-Donner home in which my mother-in-law has posted on the side of the refrigerator: *Lord, help me to remember that nothing is going to happen to me today that You and I together can't handle.*

By embracing this roll-with-the-punches ethos, Josephine is able to enjoy the company of her grandchildren; she is able to stave off panic when, for instance, Devin—a lad with, as I've mentioned, a precociously large digestive tract—creates an occlusion in the powder room commode twelve minutes before the arrival of dinner guests. Aside from such rare, minor crises, the kids have a ball on these ski vacations. Until it is time to ski.

Laura has very much looked forward to the first family vacation of the Experiment. "Soon you will learn the secret," she confides, "to which all mothers become privy: Mom never gets a vacation."

Lying in bed on the morning of our departure, she begins a subtle interrogation. She is using the Socratic method to draw from me all the tasks I must tick off before we hit the road.

"Put the dog food in a big Ziploc for the kennel?"

"Yes, but what else?"

"Pack for kids?"

"And?"

"Snacks for the car."

"Keep going."

The answer to which I am being guided is: Clean the house for (and leave cash in an envelope for) the house cleaners, who will arrive in our absence on Tuesday morning.

One of Laura's conditions for allowing me to "replace" her was that we not give up the nice Brazilian couple who clean our house every two weeks. "For an hour or two, twice a month," said Laura, "our house does not look disgusting. I cannot bring myself to give that up." She got no argument from me, which meant that I got an hour-long tutorial called How to Clean for the House Cleaners, which included such tips as "When you're tidying the back bathroom, be sure the toilet is flushed." Pause. "Our children can be so disgusting." For the six months I carry it out, cleaning for the house cleaners will never stop feeling silly.

Cleaning for the cleaners sets me back a solid hour and half. Willa is exceptional in so many ways. She is a voracious reader, a talented writer, and a nascent cartoonist. She is a kind child with a clearer idea than I, too often, of right and wrong. On the debit side of the ledger, after a day of upholding those exacting standards at school, she can be inclined to lower them at home. Willa is an Oscar Madison–caliber slob; her room, a landfill of detritus so dense that the only solution was to throw everything in a thirty-three-gallon Hefty bag and stash it in the Rat Room. (Adjoining our garage is a room that, before we wrote a fat check to have it professionally vermin-proofed, had been the refuge of, yes, rats.) Bad news, Barbies: Willa seems to prefer her Bratz dolls—the slutty ones with names like Yasmin and Cloe. The demoted Barbies will be taking up residence in the Rat Room, along with the Raggedy Ann and Andy that Willa has not thought about in three years. You'll want reading material, so here *The Kingfisher Book of Children's Poetry,* Willa's second-grade yearbook, and a half dozen Berenstain Bears books. Enjoy!

House cleaned, car packed, dog deposited at the Country Inn (for $25 a night, they better put a mint on his pillow), we motor east. Let me tell you about our first morning in Tahoe. I rise before seven, make breakfast for the kids, make lunch for the kids, then get them in their ski clothes. (Six words—*get them in their ski clothes:* one hour). Once at the resort, of course, there is the additional, bonus servitude of stooping to force their feet into ski boots, the hand-to-hand combat with the boot buckles, the carrying of their skis and poles (in addition to one's own) the 1.5 statute miles from the parking lot to the lift, plus assisting them, once the suspenders on their snow pants are snapped and their ski jackets zipped, in unsnapping and unzipping same when the children announce, as is inevitable, that they need to pee.

Adding to the challenge is the fact that you are performing these tasks at a mile and a half above sea level, where the scarcity of oxygen in the atmosphere has been linked to an increased inability, on the part of young children, to listen, focus, obey, and otherwise not piss me off fifteen different ways before breakfast.

Of course, once you hit the hill—once you get those lovable urchins clicked into their bindings—it's all worth it, right? That's when the smiling starts, and the fruits of one's labors are reaped. Right?

We are on the Hot Wheels chairlift by ten o'clock. Not a great start, but we have all week to get the drill down. A storm has dumped two feet of snow on the Sierras over the weekend. Now the sun is out. We download without incident. The day is pregnant with promise.

Weasel is a blue run, moderately difficult. By the end of last winter, the kids were chewing it up and spitting it out. This morning, on their first run of the season, they're rusty. The new snow has been carved into moguls. By the end of the week,

Weasel will bore them. This morning, they can't link a single turn. Willa melts down spectacularly, sobbing in the snow, railing at our stupidity, telling us it was our fault for taking them down this hill.

"You're right, of course," I agree, leaning toward her. "I had no idea that you'd be so much worse than you were a year ago."

I regret saying it even before Laura wheels on me, incredulous. "I don't think that tack is what the situation calls for."

It takes us twenty minutes to get down the hill. At the bottom, my daughter collapses again. She has sunscreen in her eyes, her ski pants itch, she is so hungry she's "about to faint."

Laura Hilgers, food cop, recognizes her cue. "What did you eat for breakfast?" (Laura was showering, then doing yoga, then blow-drying her hair and applying cosmetics while I fed and dressed the children, so she genuinely doesn't know.)

"Honey Nut Cheerios," says Willa.

Addressing a distant granite peak, Laura remarks frostily, "These kids have got to get some protein in their breakfasts."

This is why our Ski Week is off to such a spectacularly poor start. Some nincompoop gave them cereal.

We split up. Laura takes Devin to the Meadow chair, a green run. I buy Willa chicken strips and a Snickers, and she metamorphoses before my eyes from vicious Harpy-in-training to lovable third grader. I apologize for my mean-spirited remark on the mountain. "Sometimes when grown-ups know something is their fault, it makes them even angrier," I explain.

A couple of runs later, I lose her. I sit down to get water from my backpack, motioning for her to pursue Laura and Devin, whom we'd rejoined. Assuming she'll catch up to them, I take a different run to the bottom. But Laura and D. aren't waiting for Willa at the usual junction, so she goes off on her own, toward the wrong lift. After ten minutes by herself, she realizes that she was lost and begins crying softly. Another mom asks her if she needs help, and Willa nods. The Good Samaritan—we never meet her—takes her to the bottom of the Roundhouse lift.

In the meantime, I take the lift called Yellow to the top. I will "sweep" the hill in search of Willa. I am paired with another "single"—a tall, silver-haired man in a stridently red one-piece ski suit. "Beautiful day!" he exclaims, but his bonhomie is short-lived. Somehow, beneath our combined weight on the ancient, low-swinging chairlift, my snowboard catches an edge and turns sideways. Now trapped beneath us, my board pins the Silver Fox's skis to the lip of the lift. As the chair swings forward, he shoots out of it like a circus clown from a cannon. As I look back, mortified, he is roaring angrily at me while struggling to extricate himself from the deep snow beneath the lift.

I wait for him at the top of the hill—my back foot out of the binding, in case I need to duck a punch. He skis toward me, looking pissed. There is a moment of silence, and then I break it, apologizing sincerely. I beg his pardon. I have no idea what happened, I tell him. Nothing like this has ever happened to me before.

I can see the anger seeping out of him, so I go on. The more I abase myself, the better it feels. I nod somberly as he lectures me on the need to be more careful about the position of my board while uploading. I agree, and apologize some more. I am surprised to find myself on the verge of tears. A spectrum of strong emotions—frustration, discouragement, contrition—are roiling dangerously close to the surface. The Silver Fox is lucky I don't unburden myself of my woes right then and there: *I'm*

*up before everyone in the house, working my tail off for them, and
this is the thanks I get: they yell at me and tell me every little
thing I've done wrong. And now I can't find my daughter, and all
of a sudden I can't get on a ski lift without endangering the life
of a senior citizen guilty of nothing more than owning a decades-
out-of-date snowsuit the color of a smacked ass.*

Sensing, perhaps, my fragile condition, he begins to edge
away. "Have a good day!" I shout after him. "Watch out for idiots
like me!"

When at last, at the end of the run, I am reunited with Willa,
I again humble myself. "I'm so sorry I lost you," I say. "I'm not
having a very good day, am I?"

"It's okay, Daddy," she says, returning my embrace. "What's
for lunch?"

Lunch is turkey sandwiches, cereal bars, grapes, juice boxes,
and a conversation with Laura about anger management, and
the shitty job I've been doing with it to date.

Earlier that morning, before the veiled breakfast criticism,
Laura had interrupted my packing of the car to tell me something. I'd thought she might be planning to say, *Hey, you've been
working like a dog this morning, and don't think I haven't noticed.*

Instead she said, "It would have been helpful for you to pack
those little elastic bands we use to make Willa's pigtails."

Now, at lunch, I admit how that remark rankled. Instead of
apologizing, she smiles and says, out of earshot of the kids,
"You're feeling the resentment that ninety-five percent of moms
feel every single day, where you think to yourself, 'It's like I do
f——ing everything around here.'"

Instead of seeking to allay my anger, to defuse it, she is saying, basically, "Take a number."

The resentment is ever present, a low-grade fever that will be my companion for the foreseeable future, unless I can suddenly become a lot more Zen then I am now.

It is crowded on the deck at Alpine, where we are taking our lunch. Above us is an azure sky, to the south, the forbidding double-black-diamond Scott's Chute. Sharing our table is a tall and petulant adolescent boy who is rooting through a cooler, pulling out Glad-Wrapped sandwiches and inspecting them.

"Goddammit," he says to his older sister. "They all got mustard on 'em. I hate f——ing mustard."

He is disassembling one of the sandwiches, and I can see that it is elaborate and beautiful—far more delectable than anything I have ever made for my children: strata of lettuce and cheese heaped on a handsome serving of meat.

"Dude, you gotta be kidding," I say. I am smiling, but there is a slight edge in my voice. I have not appreciated his dropping those f-bombs in earshot of my kids. They hear enough R-rated language from me. "Look at that sandwich—it's a work of art. You should just be grateful someone made it for you."

Lowering my voice and inclining my head toward my children, I add this: "And easy with the language."

Laura looks the other way, her body language suggesting that she is not actually with me. But the adolescent tells me he's sorry.

"No problem," I say. "Where you been skiing?"

ONE OF THE BOOKS ON MY BEDSIDE TABLE DURING THE EXPERI-ment is a beautifully written, brutally honest look at raising children by Anne Roiphe. It's called *Fruitful: Living the Contradictions—a Memoir of Modern Motherhood,* and in it, Roiphe writes, "One of the reasons it's hard to express satisfaction with your life when you have children is that everywhere, every day there is anger. Not the life-threatening kind that caused Susan Smith to kill her boys, not the dark rage of depression that caused Sylvia Plath to put her head in the oven with her two babies in the house, but the quick summer storm kind of anger, the slow burn anger, the underground anger that sometimes affects what you do or say without your even knowing it was there.

"Mastering anger, not letting it trample the child, not letting it turn inward and strangle the spirit, this is a task that many of us cannot do or do not do as well as we would have liked. None of this is simple."

I need to do a better job of enjoying this time with my family. Too much of this sabbatical has been spent sulking and disliking my loved ones. I need to master the anger, to outwit and elude the dark rage. I need to have lunch with George G.

Of Lice and Men

True story: at a neighboring school district not long ago, a well-intentioned dad, a guy like me, volunteered to help out with inspections for head lice.

Upon arriving at school in the morning, he seemed strangely reluctant to leave the parking lot. When the school nurse handed him a pair of rubber gloves, he looked confused and said, "Why would I need rubber gloves to check headlights?"

I've got my first lice check tomorrow, and while I have more of a clue than that guy—*Okay, looks good, now let's see those high beams!*—the truth is, I don't really know what I'm looking for. So I throw "head lice" into a search engine and am soon delivered to HeadLice.Org—a site sponsored by the National Pediculosis Association. You can click onto an order form for the NPA-approved LiceMeister Comb (look for the gold handle; bulk pricing available) or catch up on "Current Lice and Scabies News," pediculous—er, *ridiculous*—as that may sound. Click on Lousology 101 to see scary, magnified pictures of the enemy, including a shot of a "louse hatching from egg," that sacred moment when a nit becomes a louse. While I can't find a description of what to look for in a child's hair, the site does offer to sell me the *Boss Louse Instructional Video*. Thanks a ton, guys.

It's important to remember that we're talking here about head lice—*Pediculus humanus capitis*—as opposed to the kind of critters with which, say, my brothers, might be more familiar. In the spirit of public service, however, I will allow myself a brief digression to pass along the dual remedies my father advocated for treatment of *Phthirus pubis*, a.k.a. "crabs."

"What you do," he would say, "is get a razor and shave a strip up the middle of your pubic patch." A notorious prude, he preferred not to use words like *pubic* but was willing to make an exception for the sake of passing on a vital bit of medical advice, or a good joke.

"After you've shaved the, uhh, *strip*," he'd say, "you light either side on fire. When the crabs rush into the middle, stab 'em with an ice pick."

A less painful alternative, he might continue, once his own mirth had subsided and he'd enjoyed another belt of wine from a bottle with a screw-top lid, "would be to go to the movies and deliberately oversalt your popcorn. After you've chosen a seat, spill some of the popcorn into your lap. Then, when the crabs rush up the aisle to get a soda, you change seats."

The man offered us those remedies, but never said boo about what to actually do if, horror of horrors, you looked down one

day and discovered that you had company. The unspoken message was: If this problem becomes your problem, it means that
you have been intimate with a woman outside the state of marriage, a sin for which you deserve whatever suffering and stigma
befall you.

To their credit—if you will allow me this rocky transition
from *Phthirus* back to *Pediculus*—the good people at the NPA
have worked hard to demystify their particular flightless insect.
The group's mascot, Boss Louse, has been rendered as lovably
as a pincered, bloodsucking parasite can be. The NPA seeks to
remove the stigma of head lice. It's an uphill fight. Kids who
end up with it are made to feel shame. They're pulled out of
class, marched to the office, and told to sit there until a parent
arrives to take them home. They're not allowed back in school
until they pass an inspection.

The word is that head lice was once far more common at
Brookside than it is now. The four-times-a-year lice checks insti-
tuted by Kandee Adams, our principal, have greatly reduced its
incidence at the school. Before reporting to Willa's classroom
for the actual inspection, I stop by the office of the school nurse
to pick up my "lice kit"—a pair of rubber gloves and some tooth-
picks. No, says the nurse in answer to my question, the tooth-
picks are not to be used for stabbing any nits I might discover.
They are for pushing aside locks of hair.

Between the nurse and Gloria B., our room parent extraor-
dinaire, I get a fair idea of what I'm looking for. With the child
seated in bright and preferably natural light, I will part his or
her hair, examining the scalp—especially the nape of the neck
and behind the ears—for small white or yellowish-brown specks.
To distinguish between eggs and simple dandruff, one need simply attempt to dislodge the material in question. Nits hold fast

to the hair shaft and are not easily removed. It's important to know the difference between lice eggs and what the NPA calls regular "hair debris." Last year at Brookside, a group of zealous mommies got a teeny bit carried away, deciding that every fleck and particle they found in the hair of their students were lice. Five kids were pulled from the class and sent home. None of them, it turned out, had the parasite.

Gloria performs two inspections for every one I do. I don't find a single nit, but am treated to the sight of my daughter raising her hand, answering Mrs. Leader's math questions correctly, and hearing Ruth say, "Very good, Willa." Each time, Willa looks down, then sneaks a glance toward me, to see if I've noticed.

Walking to the car, I notice a guy about my age outside Mrs. Ferrari's room. He is chatting with a third grader while expertly examining her scalp. This is George G. I've been hearing about this guy for over a month. It's come to be a refrain among the moms I've gotten to know: "You've got to talk to George." So I walk over and make a lunch date.

I try, at any rate. I think Monday at noon is good, he says. But let me get home and look at my calendar. *Damn*, I think, *this guy is good.*

MONDAY WORKS FOR GEORGE, SO WE GET A LITTLE TABLE AT COM-forts, in downtown San Anselmo, where we order in overly gruff tones—*Yeah, just gimme one of those flank steak sandwiches*—so the waitress won't think we're gay. Comforts is a MILF-orama during the lunch rush, but I'm working. This guy across the table from me, with the dark, wiry hair and the kind eyes, has my full attention. "George," I say, once we run out of small talk, "when we were boys playing with Tonka toys and Lincoln Logs and people asked us what we wanted to be when we grew up, we didn't say, 'A stay-at-home dad.' How'd you end up where you are?"

He tells me that he and his wife, Kris, both worked and needed to put their sons, Tony and Tom, in day care. Kris was an operations supervisor at an insurance company in Novato. She needed to be at work before George, so school and day care drop-offs fell to him. George had to be at work at 8:00, which was complicated by the fact that Thomas's day care center didn't open until 7:30. He would kiss his son good-bye and sprint to the truck, only to become ensnared, usually, in the morning rush. "I'd get to work at eight-oh-three, and they'd bust my balls for it," he says. "I'd say, 'Okay, I was three minutes late, now we've been talking about it for five minutes. How much sense does that make?'"

Management made his life increasingly miserable. One day, with his wife's birthday coming up, George asked her, "What do you want? Do you want to go out to dinner?"

Kris thought for a moment, then said, "Why don't you go in on Monday and quit your job?"

He did. Soon after, Kris got a promotion, increasing her salary by fifty percent. The family's child-care costs went from $14,000 a year to zero. Sacrificing George's income, it turned out, wasn't that much of a sacrifice. "The stress level in our house almost disappeared," he says. "You're parenting now, rather than paying someone else to be the parent. Their day is not longer than yours."

I level with him, telling him that my stress level remains, at times, high. And I get angry. There aren't enough hours in the day for everything I have to do.

He counsels patience. He tells me he had anger at first as well. "I had visions of all the projects I was going to get done. I was thinking, *Hey, I don't have to work. I'm at home.*

"You're home, but it's not like you're *at home, http://home*" George says. "You're the day care. Plus I was volunteering in their classrooms six hours a week. I was making four trips over the hill to Brookside every day. I've got an eight-thirty drop, then a nine-twenty. That leaves me forty minutes. What am I gonna do in forty minutes?

"Well, now I got a list of jobs I can do in forty minutes. Or thirty. Or twenty. Back then, I wasn't that organized."

I am not that organized and, for the record, will never get that organized.

"Back then," he says, "I was excited and pissed off at the same time. I wanted to think I was going to do projects. Well, guess what. You're not gonna do projects."

His life took unexpected and delightful turns. Always a baseball nut, he started coaching the sport he loved. Now he is a San Anselmo institution, and the local recreation department pays him a little to coach "Bambino Baseball"—an instructional league for the little ones just starting to play. "They call this base first base," he tells the kids, "because *it's the first base you run to.*"

"I get paid in hugs," he says. "Every spring, I teach 'em how to run the bases, I pratfall between third and home, and they all dogpile on me. How can you not be happy when you're getting that much love thrown your way?"

When does Bambino Baseball start, I ask George. It sounds like it would be right up Devin's alley. (As it turns out, Devin will be a clubhouse cancer, sitting down in the outfield like Ferdinand the Bull, refusing to stand, and inducing his fellow outfielders to sit as well.) "Hang on," says George, pulling out his day planner, which makes me feel still less adequate as a SAHD. I'd made a great show, a week or so before I took this job, of scouring the Office Depot for just the right day planner. The thing sits on my desk, buried and seldom used. The kitchen calendar is the one I work off. The whole double-calendar thing isn't happening for me.

"It's never perfect," says George. "I've still got shit on one that's not on the other. But you have to try."

He stands to share an embrace with Merrie C., a Brookside mom whose sons George has coached. Merrie is the third mother to interrupt our lunch. "Look at this," he says. "I get to hug all the beautiful women in San Anselmo. I love this job."

Our plates have been cleared by now, and George opens up a little more. "Kris and I aren't particularly religious," he says, "but we consider this the biggest blessing in our life, that one of us can stay home with the kids." What he likens it to, he tells me on the way home, "is winning the Lotto without the money."

He riffs on all the grace in his life, all the love, and ends on a slightly selfish note: "It might as well be me. You know why? Because *I appreciate it!* Look where we are, look how we live!" To our left are the redwood- and pine-studded coastal mountains overlooking the Pacific. To our right, the eucalyptus-lined ridge between us and the bay.

"There are people who have all this, same as us, who wouldn't even appreciate it," he says. "There are people who are always going to find something to be miserable about."

That is the powerful message with which he leaves me. I need to remember that this extended time with the gang is gift, not a sentence.

A couple of weeks later, George cruises past me in the traffic circle at upper campus. He slows the car and sticks his head out the window, yelling, "Hey, you—get a job!"

The moms look at me, expecting me to be offended, but I crack up.

WHILE HE MAY BE OUR BEST-ADJUSTED AND HAPPIEST STAY-AT-home dad, George isn't the school's only one. The downturn in the dot-com economy hammered the Bay Area hard, and I know a couple of Brookside dads, financial district guys, who've been cut loose. It's not that tough to pick them out in the parking lot. Once they've been out of work a couple of months, they figure what the hell, and sprout a goatee or a soul patch. You start seeing the baseball cap, because they didn't get around to showering that morning.

Some guys choose SAHD status; others have it thrust upon them. A week after George and I had lunch, I hook up with John Anderson. He and his wife, Jill, were one of the first couples Laura and I were introduced to when we moved to San Anselmo eight years earlier. In spite of his being tall, friendly, classically handsome, and successful—he sold commercial real estate in the city—I came to like him. Jill left one no choice: she was one of those bright lights you meet every so often. She was radiant, with great energy and a beautiful smile. In addition to holding down a cool job—she did marketing for Williams-Sonoma—Jill was the president of a local playground association and the secretary of Brookside Parents Club. Every day I meet women who do a superb job of balancing careers and running households. Jill left them all in the dust.

That, at least, is what I heard from Laura and her friends. I knew Jill to chat with and side-eye. It was only much later, when

I came to truly appreciate (and envy) the qualities she embodied, that I learned she was an exemplar for local working moms. She was the woman who does everything more beautifully than you, but who does it without the annoying manner of the Nicole Hollander cartoon character the Woman Who Does Everything More Beautifully Than You.

Years earlier, Jill had been diagnosed with breast cancer. She underwent chemotherapy, and the cancer went into remission. We all trusted she had beaten it for good. This, after all, was Superwoman. Yet it came back, and spread to her liver and brain. Still, she was such a stiff-upper-lip sort of stoic, never doubting that she would get the disease on its heels and finally rout it, that we tended not to doubt it either.

But one winter day in early '02, there was an ambulance outside the house. Jill was rushed to the hospital and didn't come home. She slipped into a coma, and over the course of six days did not emerge from it long enough to have the conversation her husband wishes, to this day, they'd had.

It wasn't just that he didn't get to say good-bye. John had a thousand questions—about bills, babysitters, bedtime rituals, you name it. He didn't know if she'd wished to be cremated or buried. "If I have one piece of advice for anyone in this position," he says, "it would be: No matter how difficult it may be, have the Talk. Hope for the best, but plan for the worst."

Had she known her days were numbered, Jill would have typed out, in outline form, a list of everything she handled, from birthdays to car pools to Christmas decorations to dental insurance. But she took a lot of that information with her, leaving her husband without a road map and without, really, a clue as to how to raise their two children.

He took a year's leave from his job. For the first time in his life, he started living off a calendar. "If I had a nine o'clock with some guy in the city, I could keep that in my head," he says. The sudden influx of the other appointments—Jack's baseball practice, meetings with Caroline's teachers—threw everything else out of whack. "Now," he says, "I'm lost without the calendar."

After taking a year off from work, John left the ranks of stay-at-home dads. He's commuting again to San Francisco, trying to get back by 5:30 every evening to relieve the babysitter. On Thursday, his car-pool day, he's got to be at upper campus by 3:00, so he leaves the city at 2:00 and hopes like hell "there isn't a war protest or bridge jumper"—or a war-protesting bridge jumper, as we had a couple of weeks ago.

He got prettty good at the whole staying-at-home thing, he tells me. Since going back to his coat-and-tie job, he's had a harder time finding the balance between work and home. That equilibrium eludes him.

Maybe no one finds it. That's what I'm hearing from moms I respect: my wife, my sister Lorin, and Shereen A., the librarian down the street. Of all the people we knew, Jill probably came closest.

Unfailingly polite, John asks me how the Experiment is going, and smiles as I compare it to entering the ring with the unseen adversary. I never know where the next blow will come from, I tell him. You arrange for the sitter but forget to withdraw cash from the ATM to pay her. You rush to get cash but forget to break a twenty, forcing you to overpay. You bathe the dirt-encrusted boy but forget to trim his nails, which are so long they're beginning to curl, like a mandarin's. Or you trim the nails and bathe the boy, but use the wrong shampoo—the kind that aggravates the cradle cap that has afflicted him since he was a toddler.

John is nodding sympathetically, showing solidarity, and I appreciate it, but the truth is that knowing his story, I've got some nerve to whine about anything. On the other hand, I do pick up lunch.

Please Pull
All the Way Forward

Laura descends from the office with an hour or so left in her work-day. She sees progress: a butternut squash cloven in two, each half facedown in an oiled Pyrex pan. She sees me awaiting the triple beep of the preheating oven, which will signal its readiness to receive the squash. She sees me trimming the ends from green beans while speaking on the headset to Mrs. Leader, whom I am instructing to put me down for volunteer duty on Miwok Day in mid-March. "Wouldn't miss it for the world," I say.

"Don't overvolunteer," says Laura. Her point is well taken. You'd think I'd want to get the drill down, domestically, before I started taking my love to town, so to speak. But I cannot help myself. I once did a profile of Gary Hein, who in addition to being a grandson of Mel Hein, the late Chicago Bear great, was star wing on the U.S. Eagles rugby team. "Gary," I asked, "how can you have much of an effect on the match from way out on the wing?" "You may be out on the wing," he replied, "but you're always looking for work." Those words, I later realized, doubled as a useful philosophy on life.

Not for me, obviously, but for someone without my aversion to hard work. Still and all, when a teacher or Power Mommy needs a volunteer, I tend to raise my hand. What better way to give back to our terrific little school? How better to strike deeper roots in my community? What more perfect excuse could there be to get out of tidying?

Of course, once you raise your hand a few times, put your name on a few lists, the word gets out: This guy's an easy mark. "Once they find out you're not working," says our friend Maria B., "you have no cover." Her point is valid: since the word got out that I'm game, there has been a near-logarithmic increase in the number of requests coming in.

In the past week alone I've pitched in with landscaping at upper campus and driven a station wagon–load of third graders to the Marin Civic Center. I spent an hour in Devin's classroom (they're on planets now; Mrs. Bishop cleverly puts the accent on the first syllable of Uranus); an hour in the P2 garden with Catherine Q, and attended a planning meeting for the Variety Show. (Assistant Principal David Finnane has asked me to be the chairman of the lower campus's first-ever Variety Show. "Don't sweat it," I tell Laura when she raises her eyebrows. "It's not till June.")

On Thursday, Der Kommissar Finnane calls on ninety minutes' notice and says he needs a sub for yard duty. Despite feeling slightly taken advantage of, I show up. I have to get

Barbara, one of the playground monitors, to tell me what the hell yard duty consists of.

When a child finishes lunch, she explains, the child raises his or her hand. The yard-duty volunteer then inspects the child's lunch. "If it's obvious they haven't finished, you ask them to eat a little more."

After ten minutes, a boy named Michael asks to be excused. "But you haven't touched your sandwich," I say.

He comes right back at me: "You wanna feel how disgusting this is?" The beverage his mother packed for him has leaked. The bread in his sandwich is as saturated as a kitchen sponge.

"Dude, that is disgusting," I say. You are free to go.

After monitoring a kickball game for fifteen minutes, I can help myself no longer. I cut into the batting rotation—my body language saying, *If any of you seventy-pound people has a problem with that, I invite you to try doing something about it*—and motion for the kid with the ball to roll it my way.

It was a ridiculous cookie, a madeleine, that transported the main character in Proust's *Swann's Way* back to his youth. My madeleine is a ripe red dodgeball. I am dimly aware, as I kick through the ball, George Blanda–style, of the danger that it might hit knock some six-year-old waif off her feet as it comes screaming back to earth. That, frankly, is a chance I am willing to take. It is a chance I am willing to take because I love kickball. It wasn't until I started spending time on elementary school campuses every day that I realized how much I missed it.

I am overly anxious that first afternoon. I pop up to what would've been left field, if I were still in eighth grade. That was the year I peeked as a kickball player; the year I unleashed a throw from shallow center that was rising like Bob Gibson fastball when it caught the foolhardy Phil Birkhead—trying to score on me from second on a single!—behind the left ear, knocking him off his feet and reducing him to tears. Yes, I was sent to the office. No, Birkhead didn't score.

Because my opponents are eight years old or younger, they are playing in. They don't know any better. My moon shot sails over their heads, caroming with a rubbery twang off the wall of the music room before it is corralled by the left fielder. I run the bases slowly, ensuring that the cutoff man will have a chance to nail me between third and home. When he does, pegging me squarely in the lumbar region, I roar with feigned outrage. Everyone is happy. After this, I have no qualms about stealing occasional at-bats in kickball games. I never hit anyone on the fly, and, like Phil Birkhead, I never score.

THE ONLY VOLUNTEER WORK I DO THAT MAKES ME TENSE, THAT feels like work, is manning the traffic circle at upper campus. Neumann Circle, named for a former principal, is a scenic little sphere of campus. It bears the flagpole, lovingly manicured shrubs, and a pair of plum trees throwing shade over an Elysian green infield. I see it as different things at different times: now a karmic circle, rewarding patience and selflessness; now a centrifuge that spins to the surface all the unflattering qualities we exhibit when the morning is going poorly and/or we have not yet had caffeine.

Every September, at Back-to-School Night, parents are lectured on drop-off and pickup rules and etiquette. They are told, early and often, to pull all the way forward. The more cars lining the circle to discharge their precious cargoes, the less time anxious parents behind them spend waiting. *Pull all the way forward.*

It sounds so simple, doesn't it? And yet, even though it is frequently repeated in the bulletin, parents continue to screw it up.

That's partly because by the time they arrive on campus, by the time they have cruised up Butterfield and taken the tight right on Green Valley Road, which feeds into the circle, they are not thinking about smooth traffic flow. They are reflecting on this paradox: Why, if I love my child, will my mood improve drastically the instant he or she is out of the car?

I empathize, people. We spend the minutes between 6:30 and 8:05 making breakfasts and lunches for everyone but ourselves; pleading with ingrate offspring to at least have a little nibble of their sausage or scrambled eggs, so they'll have something in their stomachs for school. We beg them to make their beds and put on their clothes, apologize to them for having to apply sunscreen. For my part, I have lost my temper at least once by 7:55. Guaranteed. What I have not done, usually, is shower. (I have noticed, and been helpless to reverse, a gradual decline in my hygiene over the course of my temporary motherhood. In the past, if I noticed on campus a warm-ups-clad mom with unwashed hair, I would think, *Well, isn't that a little sad—she's given up.* Nowadays, that frazzled hausfrau is me.)

On the way to school this morning, darling Annie Maguire repeats this snippet of *Shrek* dialogue thirty times:

"Donkey, why don't you go away?"

"Me, Shrek? I'm making waffles!"

Thirty times. At least. Something about those lines—maybe the mention of waffles—mesmerizes her.

"Annie, how long are you going to keep saying that?" I ask with a forced smile. I am ready to chug lye.

"I want to get it into your head," she answers.

Even though I have an excuse to flout the rules of the circle—

I'm sorry I cut the line, fellow parents; I was driven to temporary insanity by an eight-year-old girl—I do not. I respect the rules. If this thing is going to work, we must all do our part, must subvert our own individual concerns, issues and problems—*I have a nine o'clock meeting in Novato! . . . My ferry to the city is leaving in twenty minutes!*—for the greater good. Which leads me to an unavoidable conclusion:

This thing is not going to work.

In a perfect world, the circle would operate like this: a caravan of four or five cars pulls into the circle. The children disembark, the cars pull away. Four or five additional cars pull up. Repeat, until rush hour ends and classes begin.

Should you arrive at an empty circle, pull all the way forward, so that more cars might fit into the circle behind you.

While you are waiting on Green Valley Road to access the circle, do not swerve into the left lane, passing the cars whose drivers are abiding by the rules, in order to improve your position in line.

When the drive is, at long last, clear, do not pull up to the closest stretch of sidewalk *and stop!* Have an atom, a neutron, a quark of consideration for the motorists idling behind you, waiting to discharge their writhing cargo. Pull all the way forward, even if it means Little Lord Fauntleroy will have to walk an extra twenty yards to his classroom. He'll live.

Do not, once you are curbside, *park your car and leave it,* setting a roadblock for every parent behind you, creating an occlusion that will stretch, depending on how long you visit with your friends or your child's teacher, all the way out to Butterfield Drive.

There is not a morning I visit Neumann Circle that I do not see at least a few of its rules being flouted. It never ceases to

Pickup Dad is our most consistent repeat offender. In the Parking Circle Deck of Cards, he is our ace of spades.

There is hope for a brighter tomorrow. Money has been requisitioned. Next year, signs will be posted. "What will the signs say?" I ask Kandee. Her answer is almost truthful: "They will say, 'Please Pull All the Way Forward. Duh."

Birds, Bees, and Bullet Trains

Erin Go Barf: Devin not himself on this St. Patrick's Day morning, announcing that his head feels "a little bit dizzy, like the last time I was sick." Sure enough, he has a fever of 102. On my way home from dropping Willa off at school, I pick up some crackers and "healthy" soda.

He puts away a can and a half of that stuff, then sits up suddenly during *Rugrats*—when Dad is Mom, sick kids watch cartoons—and expels a Bull Connor–firehose stream of still-carbonated vomit halfway across the living room. Devin is terrified of throwing up (he's sure he's dying, that he will huck up actual organs) and notorious for getting little to none of his vomit into the can. This morning is no exception, as I wrestle him into the bathroom in time for the last feeble rivulets of gak to fall into the bowl.

"That's funny, Dev," I tell him, once we're back on the couch. "Our people usually throw up the morning *after* St. Paddy's."

When ill, I've noticed, D falls apart, shuts down, foresees Armageddon. This behavior, as much as his innate proclivity to cup his genitalia and slump catatonically on the sofa while watching TV, seems gender specific and hardwired into his genes.

While sick women seem to shunt aside their misery and woe, afflicted men wallow in it. I have a vivid memory of chancing upon my mother while she was in distress in a bathroom in our Pittsburgh house. She was throwing up, but doing it quietly and clinically. It struck me as sad that no one was there to minister to the ministerer. Of course, it would probably have struck me as ludicrous that dinner would not be served on time that evening. Unless it was one of her occasional, crippling migraines, my mother, like most mothers, muddled through, illness be damned. If she didn't do her work, it didn't get done.

When guys get sick, it's somehow different. And why shouldn't it be, since the world is, after all, ending. Even the most stolid among us in good health become drama queens when ill. In the throes of our fevers, congestion, nausea, we seek to assure all who behold us that no human being has ever been quite *this* sick, has ever been required to endure such distilled agony. Such is the attitude copped by Devin in the hour or so after he blew chunks on Monday morning. He sprawled on the couch, mouth agape, in an attitude of abject misery—one of the damned in Michelangelo's *The Last Judgment*.

He drifts off, then awakens around lunchtime chipper as a chipmunk. His mood is improved by a tape I am airing: a History Channel special on aircraft carriers, followed by a special on the evolution of the bullet train. Life is very, very good. "Hey Dad," he says. "Since I threw up most of my soda, can I have some more?"

"How do you know it was soda you threw up," I ask, just to be contrary. Like I said, you could still the little bubbles of carbonation in it as it arced toward the floor.

"Because it tasted kind of good," says D.

When the specials are over, when America has won a costly but decisive victory in the Battle of Midway, I suggest to Devin that three and a half hours of uninterrupted television are probably enough. He nods, too tired to argue the point. He is happy to vegetate, while I place a palm on his forehead—ostensibly to monitor his fever but in reality just to stroke the soft skin of this little person whom I tell, as he drifts off, "Do, even though you're not feeling well, you're a very special boy."

His eyes do not open as he answers, in perfect seriousness, "I know."

I'LL COOK AND CLEAN FOR LAURA. I'LL PICK UP SUPERABSORBENT, organic tampons at the health food store for her. But there are some things I cannot do for Laura, will not do for Laura. When the brown Amazon.com box arrives on our front step, both our children, healthy Willa and ailing Devin, are drawn to it like moths to a flame.

Laura is on her own.

"Can I open it?" says Willa, seizing the parcel.

"No," says Laura, appearing slightly flustered. "It's something for me."

"What?" comes the dual rejoinder. "What is it?"

"Something for work," says Laura, who is such an atrocious dissembler that I ask her, the moment Willa is out of earshot, what's *really* in the box. Laura has decided that the time has come to bring our daughter up to speed on, well, sex. And reproduction.

Laura wants to have the Talk with Willa before the child starts picking up stray morsels on the playground. It seems far too early to me, until I remember that I got the Talk in fourth grade. After dinner one evening, the old man drove me to a sporting goods store at the Fox Chapel Plaza to purchase my first jock-strap. On the ride home, I stared ahead into the darkness as he explained, straining to sound matter-of-fact, how there had to come to be, ahem, eight Murphy kids. Sometimes, he said, to show each other how much they love each other, man and a woman—I should say a husband and wife—join together in the act of, ahem, love.

I was no help, alas, during my father's oration. I remained mortified and mute as he spoke clinically of spermatozoa, eggs, and fertilization. He made a point, before closing, to toss in a stern warning against the spilling of one's seed. "That's not what it's there for," he intoned.

Hey, the man tried.

After dinner (Alaskan salmon filet, asparagus soup, roasted potatoes), Laura hurries through the dishes. She's promised Willa a "surprise." The women disappear into Willa's room, where a surprise, indeed, awaits.

The box contains not a toy but, rather, a copy of *It's So Amazing! A Book About Eggs, Sperm, Birth, Babies, and Families.*

"This is boring!" shouts Willa, whose voice conveys more anxiety than ennui. My tidying brings me toward the back hall, where I cannot help but overhear Laura reading from the book: "Most kids, but not all, are curious about how such an amazing and wonderful thing could possibly happen."

"I'm not!"

Laura begins the session by inviting Willa to share what she already knows on this subject. Willa takes the Fifth. After they've read forty pages, including chapters titled "Egg + Sperm = Baby," "What's Sex?," and "The Amazing Sperm Trip," Laura calls it a night, enabling Willa to at last emerge from under her covers. Now, says mother to daughter, was there anything you wanted to ask me?

Again, no response. Willa will process this information on her own time. In the meantime, I suggest to Laura, as we turn down the bed that night, let's reinforce the lesson by leaving our door wide open as we mate like jungle beasts.

Both of us understand that I am joking, Laura's 8:45 P.M. conjugal cutoff having long since passed. The truth is, we each cringe for our daughter, who must now be thinking, as we have all thought in the wake of that awakening, "Oh my God, I can't *believe* my parents do that."

While the poodle is a curse on my house, a shrill and willful excrement machine, he has been useful in terms of warming the kids up to these biological lessons. Before we took Spike to the vet last month and paid $260 to have him gelded, he would attempt to mount the children, who were, naturally, curious as to his motives.

"He's trying to marry you," Laura told Devin, in the course of explaining the need for the operation. "He's trying to make a baby with you."

Devin pestered her for more details. "Babies are made when the man puts his seed inside the woman," she said.

"You mean Mr. Maguire put his seed inside of Mrs. Maguire nine times?"

No answer.

"And Daddy put his seed inside of you two times?"

"You mean this year?" I said from behind the newspaper. "Not yet. But it's only February. Give me time."

Life During Wartime

Stickler for verisimilitude that she is, Laura insists that I arrange all babysitting. It is yet another rude awakening. Who knew that there was not an endless, boundless supply of chipper teenage girls eager to accept seven or eight dollars an hour to feed our children, then play Clue or Operation with them before shepherding them through their nightly ablutions—including rinsing the gunk off D.'s retainer—and into bed? Until you have to make those calls yourself, until you have to listen while the teenage girls come up with transparent excuses to blow you off—*I have tons of homework . . . I have a flute recital coming up*—you don't realize what a pain in the arse it is.

(While I am Mr. Mom, I retain many dadly duties, such as Dropping the Babysitter Off, that always awkward interlude during which the body language of the young woman in the passenger seat is saying, *Just a few more blocks now, just a couple hundred yards and I'll be out of this car!* I like to defuse the tension with a bit of levity, a rhetorical question along the lines of "So, are you in, like, a *huge* hurry to get home?"

Not really. But you can see my point: dropping the babysitter off should always be the woman's job, even if she does then get a late start applying unguents such as Renova to the imaginary wrinkles around her eyes.)

Jackpot! I have Kayla lined up for March 19. She is awesome, fourteen going on twenty-four, hip, smart, and funny; plus, the kids love her. It's all good. Laura and I are headed into San Francisco, to the Carnelian Room in the Bank of America building, for a speech by Rebecca S. Chopp, the new president of Colgate University, our alma mater. Laura was a couple of years behind me. She was one of the best-looking women at the school, but she knew it, unfortunately, and for two years would not speak to me other than to let me know, at parties or in bars, that she found my writing in the school newspaper forced, sophomoric, and overly reliant on adjectives. Three years after I graduated I ran into her in New York City. By then her standards weren't quite so rigorous, and she agreed to have a drink with me. We argued, fought, laughed, and were married within two and a half years. She still thinks I use too many adjectives.

To kick off her talk, the president calls for a moment of reflection, noting that the first American missiles have begun falling on Baghdad. A pall falls over the gathering—a palpable sadness, which until then I alone had been feeling, on account of being the only person in the Carnelian Room wearing jeans. So I stand after the speech, self-conscious, underdressed, willing myself to go slow with the Merlot as I mingle with more formidable alums, "players" decked out in the raiment of success: pinstripes, power ties, gin blossoms. When the conversation comes around to what I'm doing, I begin to explain that "I've taken some time off work to be a stay-at-home dad," and their eyes start wandering. You can almost hear them thinking, *No need to waste a business card on this guy.*

Back home that night, Laura and I watch as reporters on CNN speak of a U.S. intelligence coup. The Pentagon had received a tip as to where Saddam Hussein was bunkered, and dropped three dozen Tomahawk missiles on his head. The possibility is breathlessly floated that the regime has been "decapitated" before the war has even started.

Umm, not exactly.

We quickly establish our war routine. We put the children to bed and tune in to CNN. Aaron Brown checks in with Wolf Blitzer or Christiane Amanpour. He listens to their report, follows up with a couple of questions, and sign offs with a mildly cloying "Stay safe."

Yes, there are some 640 reporters "embedded" with our troops in Iraq. But come next football season, the Michigans and Ohio States and Kansas States of the world won't let me talk to players four days before the game. Because, you know, it might negatively affect their ability to grasp and recall the complex game plan. These embedded reporters are getting access to generals and colonels in the middle of a war, and I can't talk to the Wolverines' f——ing long snapper on a Tuesday before the game.

Think these coaches take themselves a little seriously?

ON ONE OF THE FIRST EVENINGS WE SETTLE IN FOR OUR NIGHTLY, you know, war fix, Aaron throws it to a young correspondent named Kevin Sites, who appears to have stepped out of an Abercrombie & Fitch ad. His shoulder-length mane ripples in the wind as he reports a major explosion to the southwest, and he makes frequent references to his Kurdish sources. I feel studly when I get an NFL scout on the phone, and here is this guy breaking bread with real rebels. My sense of inadequacy, never far from the surface these days, is fed by Laura's reaction to Mr. Sites.

"My word," she says. "He is beautiful." While my love for her is an all-consuming flame, all but blinding me to the existence of other women, I understand that not everyone is capable of such purity and depth of emotion. If Laura has a bit of a wandering eye, that's okay, as long as it's only her eye that wanders. Still, I just don't see all the fuss about this hair farmer. The guy looks nothing like me.

What I find interesting is the barely concealed euphoria of the embedded reporters. A week or so into the war, one correspondent can't help burbling to Brown, "It's great fun!"

Of course it is. In time, the body count and the privations of war will wear them down. But in the beginning, during the charge toward Baghdad, all but the most hard-boiled of the correspondents exude Kent Dorfman–like eagerness. And why shouldn't they, I think as I stand at the kitchen counter, making tomorrow's lunches. This is the pinnacle of their careers. This is why you go into journalism, to cover history as it unfolds.

And then there is this gonzo journalist, cutting the crusts off his daughter's turkey sandwich, because he forgot to cut them off yesterday and was sternly rebuked.

One of the embedded reporters is ABC's Bob Woodruff, who graduated from Colgate with me—he was an impossibly dashing lacrosse phenom—and is now a rising star at ABC News. Currently he is riding a tank with a battalion of marines somewhere outside Baghdad. In addition to seeing Bob on TV—he rules— we are getting periodic e-mails from his wife, Lee. The hardships Laura endures during my five-day absences—or even the Tours de France and the Olympics, which take two weeks or more— are beggared by what Lee is going through. (I don't think Bob's having much fun, either, but I'm representing for the moms this time around.) She's looking at four months with four kids— including twin girls—sans husband. On those occasions when he can phone home, Bob describes hideous windstorms that blow fine sand "into every orifice of his body," of no water for showers or laundry, and of sleeping knees-to-chest in tanks with a dozen marines. He tells her about the twenty-three-year-old marine in his division who stepped on a land mine.

Lee doesn't complain in the e-mails, but it's clear there is an intense strain on her. She describes her life as "a kind of parental triage: packing the lunches, unloading the dishwasher, explaining long division for the fifteenth time, cooking dinner while plugging in a video . . . I'm reaching so hard for normalcy that my teeth hurt."

I feel a kinship with her—she is describing my new life!— but the grunt work I abhor she embraces, for it keeps her mind from darker musings. "It's impossible to succumb to your fears," she writes, "when there's so much to do, so many needs to tend." Things don't feel normal for me yet, either. But after reading Lee's accounts of her life during wartime, I never felt quite as oppressed or put upon.

Which is not to say I am not both of those. We're having some bad mornings around here. Today, D. begins melting down the moment his freakishly large feet hit the floor. He refuses to get dressed. "Fine," I say, "I'll take your ass to school naked."

He gets dressed. He knows there's steel behind the threat; we once dropped him off at preschool in his Scooby-Doo briefs. (This was before he made the philosophical decision to eschew underwear and "go commando" for the rest of his life.)

I make him fried eggs, and he refuses to eat them, saying, "I didn't want a fried egg, I wanted the kind of egg where it's still shaped like an egg"—i.e., hard-boiled. Maybe I misunderstood him. Since he started wearing the retainer, the kid speaks as if he's got a mouthful of marbles. Even if I did, I'll be damned if I'm going to cook any more eggs. He fights me on the sunscreen, fights me about getting in the car, would fight me if he were on fire and I was trying to put it out.

No help today from Laura; she takes off at 7:40 two mornings a week for yoga. "Yeah, that means you're on your own for *twenty whole minutes*," she says, trying to make light of the hardship. But she knows the truth. She knows those twenty minutes before one must force-march the children toward the car are often the day's most desperate moments, the moments during which bayonets are affixed, during which Willa, immersed in a book, becomes deaf to entreaties to brush her hair and put on shoes and socks; during which Devin hardens his determination to disobey.

I am so mad at him this morning that we exchange not a word in the car on the way to school. Driving past my usual parking spot, I pull up to the path down which we usually walk hand in hand. Most days we stop and inspect the upper branches of the majestic oak lording over the path. We look for squirrels.

On this toxic morning I say to Devin, "When your behavior improves, I will start walking you to school again. Today, you're on your own." There has never been a day I've not walked him onto campus. I see other parents drop their kids off and drive away, and I think, *Wow, they must be in a serious hurry.*

He gets out of the car grim-faced. I pull away without looking back. I have to fight, hard, the temptation to go around the block, park the car, and walk after him. Instead, I drive home wondering what it says about me that a six-year-old can reduce me to a trembling rage that stays with me for half the morning.

LAURA BATHES THAT EVENING, THEN SAVES THE WATER FOR ME. (funny, I have no qualms about using her old bathwater. Yet when I offer her mine, she's never able to completely conceal her revulsion.) From my refuge in the tub, I confess to her that I am experiencing a euphoria deficit. With all this extra time in the bosom of family, I say, I was looking for a few more transcendent moments, was hoping to be awash in more bliss than this. Lately, I'm either chewing someone's ass out or getting my own chewed; I am exasperated, snappish, tendering frequent apologies.

"The job is inherently frustrating," says Laura, "because so much of parenting is reaction. You're not following through on plans so much as you are reacting to emergencies."

"It's that," I allow. "But it's also the shameful secret behind why families vacations are so often disappointing. Once you're forced to spend this much time in close quarters with your loved ones, you remember what objectionable people they are." I smile, to let her know I'm joking.

Am I joking?

The next day begins a concerted search for the joy in this

journey. Under the heading "Where Is the Joy?" I begin compil-
ing a list. In two days I run out of notebook space. A sampler
of reasons I'm glad to be a SAHD:

- The joy in unsolicited embraces from Willa, who is reaching
  that age where she objects to PDAs (Parental Displays of
  Affection) and is apt, someday soon, to start making me drop
  her off two hundred yards from school—but surprises with
  fierce hugs at unexpected moments.
- Snuggling with Devin. At bedtime, I read him a book, then lie
  next to him while he nods off, never taking it personally when,
  in the fitful throes of presleep, he clubs my trachea with a
  forearm.
- Walloping kickballs into the ionosphere.
- Driving home from the Panda Room, where the children get
  haircuts. By trimming Willa's bangs, the stylist "opened up her
  eyes," as they say. I keep sneaking peeks at her in the rearview
  mirror, she is so beautiful.
- Popping into the Roastery every morning after the school drop-
  off, chatting up the other moms, watching the baristas work.
  A heat wave has induced the caffeine vixens who make our
  lattes to don tops that are sheer and brief and expose their
  midriffs. Good for them. I wouldn't want them to be uncomfortable behind the counter. This morning the redhead ladled
  the foam into my latte in the shape of a little heart. I noticed
  that the guy behind me didn't get a heart—he got more of a
  symbolic fish, like the kind fundamentalist Christians put on
  their cars. I don't think I'm reading too deeply into the matter
  when I conclude that the redhead probably digs me.
- Volunteering in D's classroom, helping kindergartners finish
  the sentence "The sun is good because . . ." Out of the corner

of my eye I watch Devin "write," with Jan's help, "Becuz it maks my straberys gro." (We've got a small strawberry patch in the side yard that D treats as his private stash.) I like having this ringside seat as the light starts to go on for him. It's not so much a switch being flipped as it is a rheostat being slowly turned up—but it's happening, and I'm around to see it happen.

- Rapping lightly on Willa's closed door around 9:40. Funny, the room was pitch-dark, yet she is sitting bolt upright. "I hope it's a good book," I say. She pulls a flashlight from under her covers, illuminating a mischievous smile. "Go to sleep pretty soon," I say, "or you'll be cranky in the morning."

WILLA IS EXCITED BECAUSE WE ARE COMING UP ON NOT JUST HER birthday but her birthday week. Like any self-respecting child in this, the nation's second-most-affluent county, she would be insulted by a birthday celebration limited merely to the anniversary of her birth. So, in addition to our family party, held on her actual birthday, I have planned a party for her friends for Friday, April 4. It will be held at the Class 5 climbing gym in San Rafael. I bought invitations a month ago. I picked them up at one of our precious boutiques in downtown San Anselmo. The cards were blank, but they came with an adorable little "show" envelope, featuring a little cornflower button, to be tucked inside the real envelope. They set me back $22.50.

"Jesus," says Laura. "I usually spend about five bucks on invitations."

"Yeah, well," I counter, "we saved money on my birthday." Pleading exhaustion, penury, and a dearth of gift ideas, Laura had given me squat for my forty-second. I was not saddened by this so much as I was made keenly aware of a double standard: if I'd ever ignored her birthday that comprehensively, I'd still be bringing her tissues to stanch the flow of hot tears.

On the cards, I print out the what, where, and when of Willa's party. On the flip side, I glue a color photograph of a woman ascending a sheer rock face. Between the card, the faux envelope, the waiver, and the SASE in which parents are instructed to return it, it is a bulky, unwieldy mailing. I send out nine invitations; six mystified moms call with questions.

UPON OUR ARRIVAL AT THE CLIMBING GYM TWENTY MINUTES EARLY, a very concerned, very childless twenty-something employee confronts me, saying, "You know your reservation wasn't until four o'clock, right?"

I explain that the girls got out of school at three o'clock, and that we drove over as slowly as we could. If this is a problem, I say, Laura and I would be happy to walk them around the cul-de-sac outside the gym for twenty minutes.

That won't be necessary, I am told. We are quarantined in the "party room" until such time as our belayers are prepared to fit the children with climbing harnesses and review the rules with them. Avril Lavigne is cranked, and a consensus is reached: the girls are starving. We have cake, but it's not cake time. I leave the quarantined area to purchase twenty dollars' worth of Clif Bars at the counter. Back in the party room, while the girls have their snack, I am swaying to the beat of an Avril tune—"Complicated," I believe—when the birthday girl informs me in a low tone, "Dad, you're embarrassing me." Yeah, well, get used to it. When we are released from quarantine, I count on the table seven Clif Bars with one or two bites taken out of them.

James O., the father of Willa's best friend, Kailey, has left work early to be at the party. James is a good friend, but let's face it: he's here under orders from his wife. Kailey has demonstrated great courage just showing up. A year ago, she fractured a bone in her foot on the climbing wall at a park near our house. In fact, it was during a playdate with Willa that she was injured. Yet Catherine and James took no legal action, a measure of the strength of our friendship.

While watching the kids assault the climbing walls—none with more agility than Kailey—James and Laura make small talk. But I can't linger. I'm working. I need to prep the party room— set the table, position balloons, hang bunting, create ambience. The climbing goes well. No child plunges from a great, or even a modest, height. Devin, the only boy invited, is feeling included. The pizza delivery guy arrives on time, and slices await the children as they reenter the party room. Candles are lit, "Happy Birthday" is sung, and Willa is aglow with covetousness: she is about to tear open nine gifts. Having served everyone else, I help myself to a slice of cake and reflect on the work and expense that has gone into all of this: the invitation fiasco, the $214 I dropped on an American Girl dollhouse (and the $35 it cost to have it express-mailed), the $25 Frida Kahlo art kit from the San Francisco Museum of Modern Art, the $180 for the climbing gym, the $70 we went through at Party America on plates, cups, and bounty for treat bags.

Something about the golden light through the window, combined with the merriment in the room and my own relief at having successfully executed a difficult project, fills me with a sense of well-being, a contentment and a certainty that I will look back on this afternoon fondly, that it will take its place in the continuum of joyous celebrations with, and of, loved ones.

Or maybe it's just a sugar rush.

Throughout my months as Mr. Mom, these moments of contentment and self-satisfaction will inevitably prove illusory and false. That light at the end of the tunnel is usually an oncoming train. As I stand chatting with James, Laura interrupts with an urgent message:

"She's about to start opening presents. You've got to keep a list of who gives her what, for thank-you notes."

For all the drama in her voice, Laura might as well be saying, "If we do not inject the antidote in the next fifteen minutes, the subject will go into cardiac arrest."

Instead, she is talking about, you know, a list. "I'll just finish my cake here," I say, "and get going on that list."

Sometimes you see them coming. But I am ambushed by this particular row with my wife. I have underestimated the depth of her convictions on the vitally important (to her) issue of making a list *as the gifts are opened.* It isn't something that can be reconstructed a few minutes after the fact. The exercise must be contemporaneous. There is no room here for a difference of opinion. This is how it has to be.

I'll keep track in my mind while I eat these last few bites, I say, trying to humor my wife, who is not, alas, giving a millimeter. She repeats her order that I put down my dessert and commence with the list making, which by this time, with James watching, I cannot do on sheer principle.

I see the sense in what she is saying. But I also know that I began planning this party six weeks ago and have brought it off with zero help from Laura, who is now in my face, telling me how to do my job. As Mike Tyson might say, "It irks me."

James saves the day, pulling a pen out of his pocket and

making the list for me on the back of a paper plate. "A good housewife delegates," I remark to Laura.

Not something this important, she shoots back, tight-lipped. This one ends up being one of our Korean War tiffs: there is no winner. Things are still frosty between us when the party breaks up, Laura heading straight home in one car, me in another, dropping off a handful of third-grade girls. They include Anna C., my freckled little friend whose mother, Deborah, had told me should she would be at a small dinner party at a neighbor's house. Would I mind dropping Anna off there?

When I walk her to the door, Anna-Lena, the hostess, insists that I come in. She and her husband, Steve, are also friends of ours. "I wouldn't think of imposing," I tell Anna-Lena, who will not take no for an answer. I end up with a glass of Cabernet Sauvignon at the table with Deborah, Anna-Lena, Steven, and another couple I have not met.

I shake hands with the other guy at the table, a dark-haired man whose gambit wants for originality. Having heard that I write for *Sports Illustrated,* he thunders, "Do you work on the swimsuit issue?" I allow as how I do. "The next time you go, do you need an assistant?"

A bit later in the conversation, it arises that Anna-Lena and Steve are Tahiti-bound.

"You've earned it," I tell her. "It's true," says Steve, who has a cool—but demanding—job with Hewlett-Packard. "I really have."

The dark-haired guy feels the need to once again flex his wit. "Oh yeah, she's earned it," he says. "It's really tough carrying those Banana Republic bags to the car."

I see Deborah's eyebrows go up. When he doesn't get any laughs, he simply assumes we haven't heard him. "Really tough," he repeats, even louder this time, "carrying those J. Crew bags to the car."

No one I know more richly deserves some serious hammock time than Anna-Lena, who spends more time as a single mother than does Laura, which is saying something. Steve travels even more frequently than I do, and when he leaves, he leaves the country. I want to tell the dark-haired guy, "Buddy, I don't know what you do"—I later learn that he's unemployed—"but I promise you that this woman works twice as hard, and could do your job better than you're doing it and be done by lunch every day."

Instead I say, with feigned cheerfulness, "So, Anna-Lena, when was the last time you were at Banana?"

"It's been a while," she says with a steely smile.

Later that evening, I can't help calling Deborah. "Could you believe that guy?" I say. We agree that we could have argued with him. But first we would have had to educate him.

Losing Devin

We are back in my world this morning, and it feels good. Equilibrium is restored, home-field advantage regained. I am bound not for the health food store or gardening duty at upper campus or some field trip, but to the Oakland airport, whose every square foot of terminal space I know the way Larry Bird knew the soft spots in the parquet in the old Boston Garden.

Here at the airport, *I* will decide where we park, thank you very much. Here at the airport, Laura will follow *my* lead as I make my unerring way to the Premier line at the United counter. Taking after *my* veteran example, she will remove her shoes before passing through security and following me to the gate, from which UA Flight 532 will whisk us to O'Hare, where we will grab a connection to Connecticut and the Wedding of the Exceptionally Tall and Gifted People. My old friend and *SI* colleague Steve Rushin (six foot five) is to take as his bride one Rebecca Lobo (six foot four), a forward for the Connecticut Sun of the WNBA. I'd last crossed paths with Rushin in February of '02, in a Salt Lake City bar that we, along with most of the Austrian winter Olympic team, were in the process of shutting down. While there will be no inebriated, cowbell-wielding Austrians at his wedding, Rushin's brothers will have little trouble picking up the slack.

I look forward to doing my part as well. I've earned a wee bender, is how I see it. I've been stunned by how much work it was, preparing for the trip. In addition to my usual duties— volunteering in D.'s class the previous Monday; taking orders from Emperor Finnane at Tuesday's Variety Show planning session; filling in for Deborah C. on Pizza Day (Thursday) handing out slices to a bunch of sawed-off, Gap-clad Visigoths at lower campus—I've busted ass to get us out the door.

I've lined up babysitting (my in-laws Josi and Al) and laid in stores for them. I've arranged to have the dog boarded—Josi doesn't do canines—and the children picked up after school. I've left on the otherwise immaculate kitchen counter a comprehensive list of menus and suggestions it was a pleasure to compose, truth be told, because it gave me the chance to show off. The note made mention of D.'s T-ball practice on Saturday afternoon, provided the number for the weather hotline, in case of rain, and a reminder to be sure that he put his mitt on the correct hand. It ended with an invitation to crack open one of the leftover bottles of wine from Laura's fortieth—this latter suggestion being, as far as I can tell upon our return, the only one they took seriously.

And so it is with a sense of well-being, the satisfaction that attends having mastered a complex logistical problem, that I belt myself into my window seat for the journey east. Nine weeks into my new life, I have no delusions of having mastered the drill. But I am gaining on it. I know how to prepare four or five dishes that even Laura can eat. I can get around the grocery store without a list. I am meeting new and interesting people—people like Perri the nose-pierced, purple-haired checkout girl at the health food store, and John, the tall and excruciatingly bashful campus custodian whom I had assumed was mute, he said so little. Finding myself walking across the playground alongside him one day, I sought to break the uncomfortable silence, asking him how it worked: Did custodians get the summer off, just like teachers? Five minutes later, he was still explaining to me the finer points of the union contract pertaining to that issue, and I was glancing at my watch.

What I've mainly been cultivating, my bond with John the Janitor notwithstanding, is a handful of girlfriends. The week before, I'd been slicing cucumbers and avocados for dinner salads while nodding sympathetically as Deborah C., who'd called to nail down a sleepover, spoke of her gratitude for her husband's excellent job and his passion for it, on the one hand, and her jealousy of its demands on his time on the other.

"That's a small breakthrough for you," said Laura as I placed the headset in its cradle. "You realize that's what women do about seventy-five percent of the time—complain about their husbands on the phone with other women."

Such minor triumphs as that—as well as not oversalting the roast potatoes, for once, and successfully taming Willa's hair in pigtails—have buoyed my spirits. So it is less galling than it might otherwise have been when, after taking in a so-so in-flight

movie with Hugh Grant and Sandra Bullock, Laura tucks her
headset into the seat-back pocket and subjects me to a performance review at thirty-five thousand feet.

"You're doing a nice job with certain things," she allows, starting with the positive. "Menu planning, shopping, cooking—
you're getting the hang of it. Good for you. Your next step in the
kitchen will be to branch out from the four meals you make, so
we can get a little variety. Cooking from recipes, making sauces,
that sort of thing.

"In general, you still need to be much more proactive. Right
now you're thinking one or two days ahead, and that's not far
enough." I can't recall a time I'd actually thought two days
ahead, but I keep my mouth shut.

"May I make a few suggestions?" (It isn't a question.) "Do a
better job of taking care of things as they come up, or they won't
get taken care of. It's the only way to fight the tidal wave. The
mound that forms at the far end of the counter near the phone—
that hill of mail and magazines and school stuff—that needs to
be cleared out at least every other day. That way the room
doesn't look as disgusting, and you're better able to stay on top
of things. You had no idea, for instance, that Devin has an animal report due."

"Two things," I interject. "One, I am aware of said animal
report. Devin is in the preliminary stages of selecting an animal.
This week he is leaning toward elephant.

"Two, while I admit that I am reacting rather than acting, it's
not necessarily because I lack organization or discipline. It could
just be my personal style." Laura is a sort of Bernhard Langer,
keeping it in the fairway, laying up, seldom smiling to the gallery.
I see myself as more of a Seve Ballesteros kind of mom—trying

to carry a two-iron 250 yards over water, scrambling for par when I end up in the sand or the woods, letting the kids eat dessert before dinner.

"Incompetence isn't a style," she points out. She is right, of course. My minor victories aside, I've spent too much of my first trimester as a kind of smoke jumper, air-dropping myself onto one domestic brushfire after another. I am setting the table with paper towels in lieu of place mats, all of which are in the hamper, it having been four days since I've done laundry. I am putting that fickle bitch of a spaghetti squash back into the oven not once, not twice, but three times before anyone can get a spoon through it. I am hand-delivering a check to the AT&T payment center in San Rafael, lest service be terminated at the end of the day; receiving notice that the children and I have amassed $45.23 in fines from the local library. These are depths to which we never sunk during the Reign of Laura. These are symptoms of entropy that must be reversed if I am to achieve, as my subjects in the world of sports so often say, the next level.

Even with her valid criticisms hanging in the recirculated air between us, I remain proud of the smoothly ordered departure I'd orchestrated. What does it say in Proverbs? "Pride goeth before destruction, and a haughty spirit before a fall."

Around the time our 757 begins its descent into Chicago, a trio of police cars line the parking circle at lower campus. A kindergartner has gone missing. For ninety agonizing minutes, the child remains unaccounted for, while cops comb the neighborhood and a half dozen teachers fruitlessly phone his classmates' parents with the same question:

Have you seen Devin Murphy?

REVIEWING NOTES I TOOK DURING THE FIRST WEEK OF MY SERVI-tude, I quote Laura as saying, "You need to transfer the dates from the school calendar onto our calendar."

I obeyed. Not that day, or week. But that month. The problem, I would later conclude, was that the Ross Valley School District School Calendar was a single sheet of paper with dates on *both sides*. The first side—the side whose dates I transferred—featured Labor Day, Staff Development Day, Martin Luther King Day, etc. The flip side, the side I overlooked, bears the headline "Additional Calendar Information." There, three-quarters of the way down the page, next to April 11, it reads "EARLY RELEASE SCHEDULE."

Instead of getting out at 3:05, D. was sprung at noon. Laura, as it happened, was all over this. Unbeknownst to me, she'd arranged with Alie, our babysitter, to walk the three-quarters of a mile over to school, meet D., then walk him home.

Before Laura made that arrangement with Alie, I'd walked across the street to speak to Carmen Maguire, who looked as regally beautiful as ever, despite the weariness that is her occupational hazard. As mentioned earlier, Carmen and Dan have nine children—a number as serendipitous as it is stunning. Dan is a fool for baseball; he presides over a collection of some five hundred baseball tomes, and used to drive around with a vanity plate that read **DH NOT**. It is only proper that he and Carmen have begotten their own side. The Maguire brood provides us with a reliable source of babysitting, and me with regular flashbacks to the sublime anarchy of my own youth, growing up with seven siblings. Carmen drives around town in a six-year-old Ford Club Wagon that seats a dozen and accumulates dents with a frequency that is accelerated each time another Maguire obtains a driver's license.

A handful of Maguire kids were down with the flu that was going around. I asked Carmen if she'd been ill. Her answer was priceless. "I don't think so," she said. "I do fall asleep whenever I sit down, but I don't think I'm sick." (My brothers and sisters always looked forward to that moment at Sunday mass when our own saintly mother, Patricia, would nod off—usually around the offertory. The eyelids would flutter, the jaw would dip toward the sternum, and she was out. She would start awake, only to nod off again. The Bobblehead Mom cycle would repeat itself until she nodded off for good, only to be awakened by our raucous laughter. "He died on the cross for you, Mother," we would say. "You could at least stay awake for Him.")

I felt a bit guilty, explaining about the Connecticut wedding, and asking her to pick up Devin after school on Friday. Of course, she said. She would be happy to.

After gathering her Robbie and Annie and my Willa from upper campus, Carmen arrived at the lower campus at the appointed hour. There was Maggie, but no Devin. Nor would there be, Mrs. Bishop told her. The kindergartners had gotten out two hours ago. After scouring the playground, Carmen went to office, where they called the cops straightaway. That's policy. The San Anselmo police were in the office inside of five minutes.

The first thing they did was call my house, where Alie did not pick up. Around 3:30, Amy K. drove over to pick up Devin for a playdate with her son, Jake.

About fifteen minutes later, the police got the bright idea to knock on our door. Alie answered it, and told them where D. could be found. They headed over to Amy's house. Asked by an officer if there was a Devin Murphy on the premises, she said yes and showed him to the side yard, where the boys were throwing metal trucks against a boulder, attempting to dent them.

"We're playin' bad guys!" explained Jake, who, come to think of it, has a lot of his father in him. The word is that, growing up in SoCal, Tom K. tended toward the wild side. Let's just say that if he'd been the one to answer the door when the cops showed up, it wouldn't have been a novelty for him.

After "interviewing" Devin—*Are you okay? Do you want to be here?*—the officers took their leave. The crisis was over, the fallout just beginning. Nothing like a few police cars on campus to get the mommies talking. By sundown Friday, the saga of the missing six-year-old was all over San Anselmo. We got calls from parents who didn't have children in the school district, but who'd heard the news through the grapevine.

Of course, we didn't get any of those messages for three days. No one called our cell phones, and no one told my in-laws, who showed up after dinner, what had happened. I went through the weekend, quaffing champagne at the Rushin-Lobo reception at the Basketball Hall of Fame in Springfield, Massachusetts, blissfully ignorant of my own recent induction into the Parenting Hall of Shame, unaware that my blunder has made us, quite literally, the talk of the town. On Monday morning, the first of the eighteen messages awaiting us on our machine is from Assistant Principal Finnane:

"Hey, Mr. Mom—Mr. Finnane here. It's quite a scene over here. Poor Carmen Maguire, who's got, what, eleven [sic] children of her own, and who was supposed to pick up Devin too, can't find him. Because he's not here. I've got Officer McGowan of the SAPD in my office, and we're wondering if you can shed any light on the situation."

Laura is kind enough, as the magnitude of my foul-up dawns on us, not to say 'I told you so'—mainly because I've already taken up the preemptive refrain: "I know, I know. You told me so."

My wife is adept at recognizing watershed moments. "This, I would think, marks the end of your honeymoon with the mommies." It had probably been fun, at first, having another dad around the parking lot and along on field trips, she says. "It's probably been nice for them to have you around. There's something sexy about a Dad who takes half a year off so he can spend more time with his kids.

"Losing one of those kids—that's not sexy."

I HAVE PROCLAIMED LOUDLY AND OFTEN, IN FRONT OF THE REAL moms, how much respect I have for them, how difficult I knew the job would be. But for all the talk, I didn't come into it with enough respect or humility. I am being taught those virtues now.

It was cute for a week or two in February, when I fouled up everything I touched. *Okay,* I thought, once getting my ass kicked on a daily basis got old, *I've got a degree from a prestigious university that is often mistaken for an Ivy League school. Now I'm going to really apply myself. I've done the Keystone Kops thing, now I'm going to be Joe Mannix. Now I want to shock people with my competence.*

Right. Next thing you know, you're stiffing Catherine, who was expecting your help at gardening. They did worm bins without me. Next thing you know, the cops are looking for your kid.

By midmorning on Monday it's time to take my medicine. I suck a deep breath, then embark on the long, slow, one-hundred-foot walk to the Maguires. I owe Carmen a serious apology.

She's already forgiven me. "It happens to the best of us," she says, telling me about the time they got halfway through Maggie's baptism before discovering that Robbie, then five, had been left at home. When they returned for him, he was fine—better than fine, Carmen recalls. He'd put a fair-sized dent in the strawberries laid out for the party.

Once the police had arrived on campus to look for Devin, Carmen had decided there was nothing more she could do. She'd loaded the kids—Maggie, Robbie, Annie, and Willa—into the Club Wagon, then sought to comfort them. "I'm sure Devin is fine," she'd said, "but let's say a prayer just to be on the safe side." She'd led them in the Angel of God prayer:

> Angel of God, my Guardian dear,
> To whom God's love commits me here,
> Ever this day be at my side,
> To light and guard,
> To rule and guide.

Dessicated and atrophied, withered and puny though my faith may be, I cannot help but be moved by this sweet little petition, offered up under those circumstances. God bless you, Carmen Maguire.

PREEMPTIVE THANKS, ALSO, TO THE GUARDIAN ANGELS WHO MAY or may not be keeping watch over us in the week that will follow. I'd put a lot of thought into where to take my offspring for spring break. It was too still too cold to camp. Disneyland was out— I'll leave it for some courageous set of grandparents to be the ones who introduce my kids to the Rat Kingdom. There was, however, a sparkling paradise awaiting us fewer than six hundred miles away, an exotic destination featuring wild animals and women with exceptionally long legs.

"You are *on your own,*" said Laura when I shared the plan with her. "I think it sounds like a nightmare." I tried not to let her negativism affect my mood while I packed for the trip. I looked on the bright side: I'll have one of the double beds in our room at the Flamingo to myself. Mom or no mom, we are going to Vegas.

Spring Break

It makes matters worse that I do not confess to her myself. Laura doesn't appreciate finding out from Devin.

He joins us in bed the morning after the kids and I return from Las Vegas. I don't know what I did to piss him off—some mornings my breath alone is enough—but he rats me out just like this:

"Daddy left us in the room at the hotel. He left us in the room while he went to the health club."

It's true, I pounded out three miles on a treadmill while the kids watched *Harry Potter and the Chamber of Secrets* eight stories above. I was back in half an hour. It isn't something I'm proud of, or something I'd do again. But was it really illegal?

Laura says it was. Laura is genuinely shocked. My fecklessness has cast a pall over the household. Laura doesn't see much difference between what I did and, say, leaving the kids in the car while I ducked into a crack house for twelve hours.

I explain that I made sure the kids bolted the door behind me. I told them not to allow anyone in the room. I know, while I tick off those excuses, that I have been inexcusably negligent, and that my only chance is to promise never to do it again and hope it all blows over soon.

"What if there was a fire?" she asks me.

"Well, our room was right over the koi pond," I say.

She doesn't laugh.

I'D HAD SUCH HIGH HOPES, GOING INTO THIS VACATION. SURE, IT was risky, taking the children to Vegas for spring break. But I'd heard (wrong) that the Strip had become kid-friendly. Paris Las Vegas had its own Eiffel Tower. There was New York–New York, Circus Circus, and Treasure Island, with replica pirate ships in Buccaneer Bay. There was a big Space Needle–looking thing.

Who knows, we might run into celebrities like William Bennett, former drug czar and self-appointed national scold—although the word is, he prefers to hole up in the "high-limits" rooms, where he can pull $500 slots out of the view of his admiring public. Even so, maybe I'd bring along our copy of Bennett's *Children's Treasury of Virtues*. If we saw Bill, we'd have him inscribe something along the lines of "Always know the house edge!" or "Don't play the milk money!"

Besides, our room was so cheap we almost couldn't afford to stay home. I'd gone online and found a rate of $55 a night at the Flamingo, where Bugsy Siegel was said to have kept up to four of his girlfriends in various suites at the same time, each one unbeknownst to the others. That, of course, was before he got whacked, on account of cost overruns at the hotel annoying his mob peers. The kids, naturally, could not have cared less about the Flamingo's colorful past. They cared that it had three pools and a serious waterslide.

It would be fun, taking my children on a road trip, even if it was over a thousand miles, round-trip. We'd learn about geography, learn about America. We'd partake of foods forbidden by their biological mother. We'd bond.

BEFORE THE BONDING CAN BEGIN I MUST SWING EAST THROUGH the Donner Pass to meet the children, who are in Tahoe with their grandparents. After dinner, I idly ask Al what route he might recommend, and I am reminded once again: you don't pose that sort of question to Al Noyes unless you've budgeted an hour. I opt for 395, which, after dropping down through Carson City, Nevada, has the good sense to wend its way back into California, through the granite massifs and evergreens of the Toiyabe National Forest and within hailing distance of the east entrance to Yosemite National Park.

By midmorning we find ourselves on the boulder-strewn banks of Mono Lake, which has been pointed out to me a hundred times by well-meaning commercial airline pilots. Even though it is the booby prize for people on the side of the plane opposite Yosemite Valley—"and those of you seated on the other side of the aircraft have an excellent view of Mono Lake"—I am thrilled to be driving alongside it with Willa and Devin.

"Usually, when I see this lake," I shout back to them, "it means I'm in an airplane and that I'm missing you both, but today we're all together! Isn't the lake beautiful?"

Willa looks up from her book, *Princess in Love,* for *maybe* three seconds. "Yeah."

Devin is playing with the toy truck I bought him at Boomtown, a truck stop–tourist trap outside Reno. After I gassed up the car, we went inside and got a taste of what lies in store: catatonic seniors, furtive-looking housewives, the vacant-eyed, the lobotomized, the undead, some smoking, all feeding slots at nine in the morning.

"This truck doesn't have pullback action," D. reports. "but I still like it."

Just north of Big Pine, I shout to a guy in a red pickup, "Is this the road over to 95?"

"It sure is," he answers. "Little curvy, about an hour and a half, but it's a pretty drive. Take a right at the Cotton Tail Ranch and you're on the way to Vegas."

He is a man of his word. Route 168, a sinuous track through the Inyo National Forest, is marked by countless signs that say dip (one, amended by a vandal, says **DIPshit**, to Willa's vast amusement). I accelerate into the dips, eliciting delighted shouts from the backseat. "I like that," sighs Devin after our fourth dip. "It tickles my wiener."

D. nods off for the last fifty miles of 168. "Devin, you missed a lot of dips," Willa tells him when he wakes up. "They weren't fun without you."

At the Death Valley Candy Co. I allow the children to purchase Ping-Pong paddle–sized lollipops, which they have scarcely dented by the time we pull up to the Flamingo.

I'd tried to get us a press rate at the Mirage. Shameless though it may have been, I e-mailed the hotel's publicity office. I'm a journalist, I wrote. Please consider giving me a press rate, and I'll mention your hotel. In the kindest possible way, they told me to defecate in my hat. "We only extend press rates to working press," a woman informed me. She wasn't finished—there was yet another reason for us not to think about setting foot on the premises. "Las Vegas is not a family destination, and we're not trying to push it as a family destination. It's really an adult playground."

At first, I was inclined to judge her harshly. I mean, lady, all you have to do is tell me you're not going to help me out with a discounted room. You don't have to tell me that my kids and I aren't welcome in your city. On the other hand, she was simply being a good publicist, staying robotically on message and making a valid point. Certainly, the sight of Roy Horn being mauled nearly to death six months later by one of his own tigers did not qualify as family fare.

We check in only to learn that Flamingo waterslide closed an hour ago. The kids allow themselves to be cheered up with room service and a pay-per-view movie. Willa orders the spaghetti Bolognese; Devin, the shrimp cocktail, which arrives early in the first act of *Harry Potter and the Chamber of Secrets*.

After making short work of his shrimp and half of my Cobb salad, then using his pajama top to wipe the food off his face, Devin leans back on the pillows of the bed he has claimed. Legs akimbo, one hand clutching the lollipop-on-Dianabol, the other down the front of his drawers, he drinks in the movie, bouncing with delight as a trio of Weasleys rescue Harry from Privet Drive in a flying jalopy. Upon arrival at the Weasleys' humble abode, Ron delivers one of his few nuanced lines of the movie: "It's not much. But it's home."

He is—they are—in heaven. This is their idea of a vacation, just as it is my first clue that we will be at cross-purposes during this break. They don't care that we're a short walk away from scores of fabulous entertainments. They take the word *break* literally—a rest, a respite.

We do okay the following morning. Willa's school friend Kendall is also staying in the hotel with her family. The classmates have a poolside reunion. The kids nearly wear a groove in the waterslide while I skim the *New York Times* and scope the talent around me. Straining the bands of their chaise lounges directly in front of me are a pair of two-hundred-pound women, both clad in bikinis they have no business wearing. One is saying to the other, "Oh my God, how did you know I was from Wisconsin?" The French Riviera this is not.

It takes only moderate coaxing to get the kids to depart the premises after lunch. A few blocks away is Paris Las Vegas, anchored by a half-scale Eiffel Tower. As we soar upward the elevator attendant, dressed like a French cop, informs us that the tower is half the size of the original, required fifteen thousand tons of steel and twelve tons of paint. It opened on the one hundred and tenth anniversary of the real Eiffel Tower.

On the observation deck, the children enjoy panoramic views of the entire valley, when they are not squabbling over whose turn it is to look through the quarter-eating telescope. Willa and Kendall admire the water fountains of the Bellagio (Virtue Czar Bennett's preferred gambling venue, I've read), while Devin is enraptured by the comings and goings of jets at McCarran International Airport. Then comes the descent, the 460-foot drop to the floor of Paris Las Vegas, whose cobblestoned floors and cafés and mimes make it "akin to visiting Paris proper," according to its promotional material, "in all its beauty and ineffable charm."

There is the added convenience, the brochure might as well have added, of not having to rub elbows with actual French people, who insist on speaking their native tongue, turn their noses up at fast food, and refuse to fall in line when we need their soldiers and money to fight a preemptive war in the Middle East.

To make the claim that anything about this theme park comes within light-years of the actual City of Lights is, of course, rubbish. That said, it's comforting to know that there is something we do better over here than they can in France: gift shops. At the clean, well-lighted Paris Las Vegas gift shop, Devin selects a foot-high Eiffel Tower replica, which to this day lends his dresser a cosmopolitan flavor.

I am delighted to spring for the gift Willa chooses for herself, a French-English phrasebook she puts to immediate use, translating her most heartfelt sentiments into another language:

"This is boring."

"Devin is stupid."

"Daddy is mean."

The act of stepping off the elevator—"MARE-SEE!" brawls a woman who complements her Parisian getup with a bread-plate-sized Silver State belt buckle—does not prevent us from continuing to sink, figuratively, to new lows. The day is still young, and I have in my possession a list of places I think the kids will love: King Tut's tomb at the Luxor; the Lied Discovery Children's Museum, a waterpark called Wet 'n' Wild, the Hoover Dam.

These suggestions are met not with enthusiasm but, rather, with insolence, disobedience, toxic recriminations. Willa and Devin want one thing: to go back to the hotel and get back on the waterslide. After that, they want to return to the room, order room service, and watch a movie. Not just any room-service order, either: the identical meals they ate the night before. ("Again?" the woman taking my order will query. "Isn't that what they had last night?" Mind you, this is a hotel with 3,626 rooms.) Not just any movie. The movie they watched last night.

Here I am ridiculing Bill (Let It Ride, Baby!) Bennett for preaching morality while blowing some $8 million on video poker and slots. The fact is, my kids are more conservative than he is. Plus, he's probably a better parent. He wouldn't leave his children alone in the room to steal a half hour in the health club, as I will do later that evening.

The next morning we are at one another's throats. I've been pushing for a trip to the Hoover Dam. "I'm not going to the Beaver Dam!" Devin shouts. (We know what he means.)

Willa is opposed, on moral grounds, to animal acts. Not long ago, we took Spike the poodle to the Marin Humane Society. Because of his exceptional cowardice, Spike's interactions with other dogs had lately been fraught with tension. So we put him in a room with a behavioral consultant. You read it right: we took our poodle to a doggie shrink. I tried in vain, pulling into the parking lot with my family and our unstable poodle, to pinpoint the precise moment when I had lost control of my own life.

During a break in Spike's therapy, Willa read some of the literature on display. Humane Society people aren't big on circuses or animal acts. "Many of these animals are mistreated," she told me during the long drive to Vegas. "They're not fed well, they're not given exercise. I read about elephants with just two yards of chain and bowls of water with dirt floating around in them! When they teach tigers to jump through flaming hoops, some of them get burned! And a lot of animals get whipped. I will not support this."

I love, and want to positively reinforce, her activism. Just not at this moment. At 9:40 A.M. I am overtaken by my first official tantrum of the trip, a Krakatoa-caliber eruption during which I go on the record as being "damn sick and tired" of the whining and complaining and threaten that if attitudes do not improve "we can get in the car and go home this minute!" Willa burrows under the covers of her bed to escape my wrath. The arrival of breakfast flushes her out. As I read the paper in the bathroom, she polishes off her and my Canadian bacon.

On our way to the pool, the children stop on the footbridge over the little stream feeding a pond in which real, live Chilean flamingos spend their days. Willa is watching African penguins sailor-dive into the pond; Devin is entranced by creatures he excitedly misidentifies as "Chinese koi!" They're Japanese koi but, again, we know what he means. While they commune with nature, I am approached by a leathery-faced man in a USC golf shirt. Despite being fifty-something, he is still pretty buff.

"You seem like a young brother," he says. I look around to make sure it's me he's talking to. He is. He needs some help. He's having trouble working his new portable CD player. After getting that figured out, we make small talk about how strong the Trojans looked, opening that can of whoop-ass on Iowa in the Orange Bowl. Gazing at Willa and Devin, he tells me what great kids I have.

"Right now," I say, allowing a bit of weariness into my voice, "I'm wishing their mom was with us."

That remark brings him up short. After a moment he says, "Hey, don't worry, man—a young brother like you, you're not gonna be alone for long." I notice that his eyes have begun to moisten. I have somehow given him the impression that I am a widower. I decide not to correct him. I mean, if he'll cry for a perfect stranger at the drop of a hat, he's probably loony enough to take a swing at me when I set him straight.

"Hey, man," he continues, "the Lord is watching over you, even if you can't always see His plan." Did I ask for this? Am I throwing off that pathetic a vibe?

He extends a fist, my invitation to press my knuckles against his—the salutation currently in vogue with the young brothers. This done, he urges me, "Go to church this Sunday. It's Easter. He died for us. Accept Him into your heart, man. I did."

"I will—I have," I stammer. At that moment, the cavalry arrives in the form of my daughter, who announces breathlessly that one of the penguins just broke wind underwater. "You could see bubbles come up from his bottom."

VOLCANIC ERUPTION II OCCURS IN AN ICE-CREAM PARLOR IN THE Mirage. We've agreed to meet Kendall & Co. at the resort's Siegfried & Roy's Secret Garden and Dolphin Habitat. Willa agrees to life her boycott of animal acts if it means seeing her friend. But Kendall and her family are stuck in another part of the city, leaving the three of us to wander around the Gardens, looking through cage bars at a bunch of nearly motionless white lions and striped white tigers.

The children are underwhelmed by the big cats, which do appear to be under sedation. I suggest ice-cream cones. After standing in line for fifteen minutes, I arrive back at the table bearing two cups of ice cream. Willa had asked for a cone, plus sprinkles. But at the Mirage, they won't put toppings on a cone. (Possibly because that's something a kid would want, and Las Vegas, you'll recall, is an adult playground.) The sight of her ice cream in a cup, not a cone, induces a tantrum in Willa. Devin, nothing if not loyal, follows suit.

After a minute of this, I instruct the children to finish their ice cream "because we are going straight back to the hotel and driving home. I can't believe I'm standing here listening to children complain about ice cream. You're both spoiled little ingrates, and the sooner I can drop you with Mommy and get some time away from you, the better."

That's a big help. Now they're crying *and* eating ice cream, and I'm thinking, *How does one transform afternoon sundaes into a bad experience?* What a hell of a parent I am.

We've all made up by the time we catch up with Kendall's family at the Stratosphere Tower. From there, we proceed to the Venetian. There, in an opulent suite with palatial bathrooms and its own little fitness center, are our mutual friends Jeannie and Adam B. Their son, Reed, is a classmate of Kendall and Willa's.

When I explained the Experiment to Jeannie a couple of months earlier, she'd just looked at me with a thin smile. It had unnerved me. "What?" I'd said. "Are you *that* sure I'll do a bad job?"

It wasn't that, she'd said. "I'm simply withholding judgment."

Since then, unbeknownst to Jeannie, I've been hell-bent on proving to her that I am up to this challenge. Both of us volunteered to drive a carload of third graders to the Marin Civic Center for *Aesop's Fables* last month. On the return, I had two boys in the middle seat, goading me into being the first car back to school. Obviously I would never compromise the safety of the children for something so meaningless. I did, however, happen to know of a few time-saving shortcuts, and was in a position to be numero uno until the final mile. As I glanced down to find a better song on the radio, Jeannie busted a move on the inside lane of Sir Francis Drake Boulevard. I could've gunned the engine, executed a quick whip-around, and beaten her to Butterfield, but it would've been tight, and illegal, and possibly witnessed by another Brookside parent.

It was a bitter pill for my boys to swallow. They were never impolite, but I could tell they were disappointed with the silver.

"That was a nice move to get by me on Drake," I told Jeannie as we stood around later with some other moms.

"I didn't realize it was a race," she said, which left me backing and filling for a moment or two, convincing the other moms that, you know, I hadn't been treating it like a race either.

Reed, Jeannie's son, has been in Willa's class for a couple of years now. He's one of my favorites, a bright kid with a big personality. When the children remove their shoes to play tag in the suite, it is Reed who first notices that something is seriously wrong.

"Oh my God," he cries out, "what's that smell? I think it's coming from his feet!"

He is looking at Devin, from whose dogs an unholy funk is, indeed, emanating. Because he refuses to wears socks, Devin sweats directly into the soles of his Payless slip-on loafers, which, by the second day of trudging the Strip, have taken on a pungency no child of God should be capable of producing.

So the game morphs into run-away-from-Devin, who, bless his heart, seems to enjoy having been singled out. When Jeannie intervenes, Reed makes a valid point: "He says he hasn't had a bath in three days!"

Now I feel the eyes of the mothers upon me. "But the thing is," I say, "he's practically been *living* in the pool."

BACK IN THE FLAMINGO, BEFORE OUR NIGHTLY SCREENING OF THE *Chamber of Secrets*—that's right, we watched it three times—I run a bath and scrub his feet myself.

We eat out, for a change. Willa sits at the food court in

Caesars, picking at her pizza slice while learning more French. ("Devin, the word for fizzy is *gazeuze,* like 'gas.' Get it?") Later, walking through the atrium at Caesars, she rattles off the names of statues she recognizes from the many mythology books she has devoured. "Hey," she says, "that's Tantalus and Penelope. I read about them." In a city built on the assumption that humans are stupid—*The house odds? They apply to other people*—she refuses to let the ethos of the place dumb her down.

We purchase tickets on the Race for Atlantis, an Imax 3D ride that actually does rock. The kids love it—almost as much as they love checking out the dancing water at the Bellagio. The hotel cranks Sinatra while the fountains do their thing. Gusting winds kick up suddenly, and we are are soaked. The kids think it is possibly the funniest thing that has ever happened.

On our way back to the room we must stop on the footbridge. There is not a single time we cross it that they are not excited all over again to see the koi, the penguins, the helmeted guinea fowl, and Chilean flamingos, which Willa admires more, if possible, than Bugsy Siegel did. In the end, we will have driven a thousand miles to stand on this bridge.

I've spent the first two days of our vacation frustrated because they've dug in their heels when I've tried to schedule an outing. Here's how smart I am: the more money they've tried to save me, the angrier I've become. They don't want to go to four shows a day. They want to be on the waterslide. They like the Jetsonian walkway that carries us to Caesars. Devin becomes tumescent, I believe, every time we step on an escalator or elevator.

Willa reads one of the signs to me. "It says koi can live sixty years, if well cared for. It says one lived for two hundred and forty seven years in a Tibetan monastery."

That was a fish who didn't take his kids to Vegas by himself.

MY KIDS ARE BARELY AWAKE AS I GUIDE THEM THROUGH THE casino at 5:45 the next morning. Only the truly compulsive are down here. No one wastes so much as a sidelong glance on my beautiful, sleep-drenched children, beyond cute with their tousled hair and stuffed animals. For this, I judge the gamblers even more harshly.

Turning right on Flamingo, my headlights catch a shadowy figure disappearing into the alley behind the bus terminal. On the overpass above I-15, we drive by a man whose possessions are slung in a garbage bag over his shoulder. All in all, I have found Vegas a depressing place to bring children, whose inheritance the city seeks to consume.

They are wide awake and fighting by the time I pull off the highway in Barstow. We need gas, I need coffee. When I emerge from service station bearing joe, the children are physically engaged, trading harmless if ill-intentioned blows. I am speaking sternly to them before I get in the car, speaking sternly as I take a left onto the access road, speaking sternly when it occurs to me that I have no recollection of removing the nozzle from my tank.

I glance left and see a silvery disembodied gas dispenser, torn from its hose and lying on the concrete like a throwdown weapon. *Oh well,* I think. *They've got my credit card information.*

I also think, not long after: *I need to start meditating again.*

Willa concludes that Boron, also just off Route 58, is a contraction of *boring moron* and surmises that it is peopled by actual borons.

I laugh, but not for long. How many of those good citizens have trashed a gas pump lately? I've long since assigned a special category of idiocy to motorists so unmindful as to pull away from the pump before reholstering the nozzle. It is alarming and humiliating to find myself in their company. It is also, I suppose, an apt coda for a spring break that seldom felt like a break.

"It's not much," says Devin some four hours later, as we pull into the driveway. "But it's home."

Nothing Left to Give

One way to regain Laura's favor is to make a dent in the mending pile. That's not a new role for me: I've always handled our sewing. My mother, whose favorite movie of all time is *The Sound of Music,* taught all eight of her children to sew. On rainy days, we made hand puppets, had shows, and sang "Edelweiss." (We didn't really sing.) I may be the only sportswriter in the country with a stash of complimentary sewing kits pinched from various high-end hotels.

Willa's comforter cover needs a couple of buttons; her dog, Max, is hemorrhaging stuffing from an open wound behind his right ear. Of greater urgency are the yawning holes in the groin of two pairs of Devin's pajama pants. My man is tough on his jammies, and not at all put out by the gaping holes over his crotch. Whereas he had been limited, in taking that crucial male inventory, to sticking his hands *down* his pants—*Everything still where it belongs down here?*—he now has a southerly ingress.

It's become a small problem during reading time. If *Eloise in Moscow* or the *The Story of Thomas Edison* takes a slow turn, Devin's hands tend to wander to the breach, and the next thing you know, we've got a jailbreak. Sometimes he is content to maneuver a ball to the opening, where it stares up at us like a sightless eye. Other times, if a show of force is called for, the Trident missile is removed from its silo.

I wince sometimes at the gusto with which the lad tugs at his, well, *area*. "Devin," Laura said the other night, as the boy deformed himself into shapes we have dubbed the Rabbit's Ears and the Shark, "you *have* to stop touching yourself there. You can only do that in private."

"And even then," I interject, "think about being a little gentler with yourself."

I tackle the sewing the day after we return, and Laura starts coming around. Of course, the quickest way to her heart is through her sensitive stomach. While she's endlessly grateful for the handful of entrées I've mastered, the reappearance of those same entrées, night after night, has begun to drive her around the bend. The night after I do the mending, she leaves the table *during dinner*—"If I don't go now the store will close," she says—to pick up a wider variety of vegetables than we have in the house. (Her nutritionist has recommended more, and different, vegetables to combat Laura's nagging cold.) This isn't exactly a vote of confidence in my cooking.

If Laura believes I've steered us into a culinary rut, then I'll get us out of it. She'd picked up some nice pork chops while we were in Vegas. I thaw those babies and take her advice on a recipe. I will prepare "Sautéed Pork Chops with Vermouth and Mustard Sauce" from *The Complete Meat Cookbook.*

I am my own sous-chef, dicing a cup of onions and two tea-spoons of garlic. I measure out a cup of sherry and a half cup of vermouth. The sauce calls for thyme and salt and pepper.

While waiting for the potatoes to boil, I whip together the kids' lunches for school the next day, then stow them in the fridge and turn to the counter, where my prepared ingredients are arranged in neat rows. *This is going to be a breeze,* I think to myself.

Which is, of course, Providence's cue to drop the Other Shoe. The recipe instructs me to put the chops in the pan when it is "hot enough to sear the chops but not burn them." The idea, I guess, is to wet your thumb, then touch the pan. If your flesh is seared, you're golden. If your flesh is burned, lower the flame. Did a "gentle hissing" emanate from the skillet or an "explosive sputtering"?

"Next," says the recipe, "sear the chops on one side for 1 to 2 minutes." Let's see: if it took me thirty seconds to locate, read, and comprehend that instruction, then find a fork, that leaves— what?—another minute of searing?

Now, directly beneath the master recipe—separated by not even a line space—is a section that begins: *To make the Pan Sauce.* I dive in and start making the pan sauce.

Mistake. I'm not supposed to be thinking about the pan sauce yet. I'm supposed to keep following the instructions for the chops, but to do that, I need to jump to page 269—the way you jump from A1 to, say, C19 to finish a front-page business story in the *Times.*

Laura realizes my mistake. There I am, sautéeing onions,

when my focus should be on the meat. "As you expand your horizons," says Laura—she is being helpful, but I am losing my appetite for constructive criticism—"you'll find that the onions and garlic are sautéed for a few minutes before the rest of the ingredients are added. It's a texture thing. Now, unfortunately, the texture of the onions is not going to be right."

It's a texture thing. I wouldn't understand.

I'm in a sour mood, mashing the potatoes. "Even though its texture has been irremediably compromised," I say to Laura, "would you give the sauce a stir?"

She doesn't like my tone. (Rereading this, *I* don't like my tone.) "You're not implying that this is in any way my fault, are you?" she asks.

"I did ask for guidance," I point out. "I mean, I'm lost in the wilderness here."

"Here's some guidance," she fires back. "A good chef reads the recipe before he starts cooking."

I grumble something about how it would be nice if she set me up with a recipe that doesn't require the chef to jump to a different page on the book, like a goddam *Vanity Fair* article.

We cook awhile in silence. It is sad to be reduced to a quarrel on this occasion. For as long as we've been an item, Laura has lamented that we never cook together. "It's collaborative, it's romantic, it's what actual couples do," she's said.

The sun comes out from behind the clouds when Laura tastes the sauce. "Omigod," she blurts, "this is so good! Whatever you did, this is delicious. You should try some."

It is *délicieux*, and a good thing that is, since the chops are the consistency of jerky. "They're a little dry," Laura concedes, "but overall, they're quite delicious." As I saw through mine, the table shakes, sloshing water over the rims of people's glasses.

Willa is working so hard to cut her chop that a sizable hunk of flesh goes overboard. Spike is on it immediately, but he seems puzzled, then alarmed by how hard he has to work to choke this meat down. I wonder briefly if anyone has ever had to perform a Heimlich maneuver on a dog.

Devin does not join us at the table. He returned from Jack's birthday part flushed and exhausted, picked a fight with us over our announced intention to trade in our twelve-year-old Jetta—the boy loves that car—then lay on the couch lamenting, to no one in particular, "No one listens to me."

Within minutes I heard his deep, regular breathing and covered him with his blanket. Halfway through dinner he stirs. I sit down and cradle his head in my arms. The damn thing weighs as much as one of those Braemar stones they toss around at Scottish Highlander games. Any residual self-loathing (over my culinary incompetence) or simmering anger toward Laura—all of it ebbs away. I catch Laura's eye. We smile.

He rises, at length, slouching toward the repast awaiting him. Watching him raven his chop brings to mind Homer's description of the short work Polyphemus made of those unfortunate sailors accompanying Odysseus. "This meat is dry," Devin remarks, between bites. That doesn't keep him from gnawing the chop down to the bone.

Afterward, while we clean the kitchen, Laura encircles my waist and draws me close. In my mind's eye, three cherries line up in a slot machine. *Jackpot!* One of the reasons you cook for Laura is that it increases the chances that she will be inclined to bestow upon you certain acts of tenderness—favors which, if you read between the lines of the Roman Catholic marriage ceremony that bound us for richer or poorer, etc.—she is pretty much *contractually obligated* to deliver. On those occasions when Laura would rank intimacy with me well down the list of things she would like to experience on a given evening, I might draw upon the lessons from the venerable sages in whose company I spend so much of my week: football coaches.

"Sometimes, honey," I'd say, "you've just gotta take one for the team."

I've gotten away from that gambit, of late, and not just because it seldom works. The truth is, since the start of the Experiment I have come to appreciate, more than at any other time in my life, the pleasures and advantages of retiring with a book before, say, 9:30 P.M., and being asleep by 10:00.

Laura expressed it differently earlier in the day. I had put out certain feelers, trying to determine whether my felonious negligence at the Flamingo would be punishable by what I call the Back—shorthand for the part of her I find myself facing when conjugal favors are not in the cards. She saw where I was going and made this coarse observation: "You don't have to worry about getting laid, since you've lost all interest anyway."

This is, of course, a gross and willful exaggeration. Despite the role I've taken on for these six months, I remain formidably virile. Endocrinologists would be confounded, I'm fairly certain, by the inordinately high levels of testosterone I produce, even as I approach my mid-forties. Despite this, it may have happened once or twice over the last three months—certainly no more than a half dozen times—that Laura has had to accept my apologies and a rain check.

Some of it, I don't mind confessing, is my appearance. Since quitting football after my sophomore year at Colgate, I'd never in my life tipped the scales past 180 pounds. Three weeks after taking over as Mom, I went through that barrier like the elevator through the roof of the Wonka Chocolate Factory. Not only am

I not missing any meals, I'm preparing ten of them a day, allowing for multiple grazing opportunities. Laura tells me she likes me with a little more heft, says I look fine, but the truth is, when I'm crowding 185, I don't feel sexy.

There is the fatigue that attends being a stay-at-home Mom, which, as I have noted, is somehow deeper and more profound than other varieties of tiredness. But that isn't the real issue here, is it? I mean, God knows I've covered myself in glory, in this arena, on little or no sleep.

To me, the most potent antiaphrodisiac is what we shall call the Mom as Infinite Commodity Syndrome, where everyone needs a piece of my time or attention, so that at the end of the day, I've done nothing for myself. But just as I crack open a book or break out the *New Yorker,* here comes Laura, playing the seductress. She is unaware, or possibly unconcerned, that I *have nothing left to give.*

Take today.

Laura was eager to take a yoga class with this happening new instructor she'd heard about in San Rafael, five minutes away. The class began at 9:00, so she bugged out at 8:15, "because you've got to be early to get a spot." In her absence, I prepared breakfast for the children, cleaned the kitchen, bathed Devin, and supervised Willa's shower; straightened up the rest of the house, drove the children to CCD, and did the grocery shopping for the week; picked the children up, drove to Toys "R" Us, bought Devin's classmate Jack a gift, wrapped said present, then took the dog for a walk.

Laura returned famished from yoga, took a long lunch, over which she read the newspaper, and agreed to drop Devin at the party. When we next spoke, I learned of a grievous error I'd made. The invitation to the party had clearly mentioned Jack *and his twin.* "We were the only family that didn't show up with two gifts," said Laura. My labors on our behalf were outweighed by this humiliation she'd endured at the birthday party.

"What can I say, I'm simply mortified," I said. "I've ruined both of those little boys' birthdays while bringing shame on our families. I must commit seppuku at once."

I did not, in fact, commit Japanese ritual suicide. Rather, I made dinner, got the dishes done, helped put the kids to bed, and concluded, once I was alone with Laura, that perhaps I did have something left to give.

In her useful *Stay-at-Home-Dads: The Essential Guide to Creating the New Family,* author Libby Gill points out that when a husband and wife swap traditional roles, it can have a dampening effect on their sex lives. For role-reversed couples whose love lives are in need of defibrillation, she suggests that they temporarily trade back. That is, once the kids are safely tucked in, the role-reversed parents can try a bit of role-playing, with the woman assuming a more reticent, submissive, traditionally female role—like a geisha, I guess, or a sorority girl in the Southeastern Conference. For his part, the man takes on his time-honored, more dominant role: *Hey, beps, that was great—all six minutes of it. How's about on your way back from the bathroom you grab me a cold beer?*

I explained this strategy to Laura, who pretended to not be completely clear on the concept: "Let me get this straight—you want me to pretend to be the dominant partner in our marriage?"

We both had a good laugh over that one.

Happy Mother's Day

My anger is beginning to well up while we are in the bookstore. We have four members of the staff looking for a particular Lizzie McGuire book for Willa, who seems to regard this mobilization of half the store's personnel as her birthright. Devin has long since found a book that interests him—and on the bargain table, no less: *Inside the Hindenburg*. He is drawn by the cover art, a portrait of the crashing dirigible engulfed in flames, panicked passengers fleeing for their lives. The boy has taken all the lessons he can, apparently, from the *Titanic* and Pearl Harbor. It is time to move on to some fresh disaster.

When time finally forces us to call off the search for Willa's book, I attempt to allay her disappointment with a box of Bertie Bott's Every Flavour Beans, a product from the Harry Potter line of products.

Devin is immediately pleading for a Bertie Bot in desperate, plaintive tones. "Pleeeeease, Willa. Pleeeease!"

"You got a book, I didn't," she replies.

"Oh, Willa, can't I *pleeease* have one?"

"Uh-UH!"

"Please, please, PLEASE!"

This fruitless exchange lasts well into our drive home until I startle both of them, and myself, truth be told, by spinning in driver's seat, channeling Jack Nicholson's character from *The Shining,* and shouting at my daughter, "JUST GIVE HIM A F——ING BEAN!"

She does, thereafter, share. But it was an inappropriate display of pique on my part. The good news is that I'm doing a much better job of controlling my anger, generally speaking. Not long ago, Laura suggested I read from a book she'd recently finished. Instead of trying to squelch my anger—that never works, anyway, says the author; it just rebounds on you like a Super Ball—I learned that I must acknowledge it, honor it, and move on. I need to recognize my anger as a legitimate response, then continue on my journey.

I have a chance to apply the new anger-management strategy at church on Sunday morning.

"All I really want," Laura had said a few days earlier, when I'd warned her that our straitened conditions would rule out more extravagant Mother's Day celebrations, "is that we attend mass as a family."

Devin selects a pew for us, but he is overruled. The pew he chooses is directly in front of the organ and has poor sight lines. I should have had my guard up. The kid has been spoiling for battle since early this morning. He'd been making excellent headway gluing lifeboats to the main deck of his model *Titanic,* and he'd wanted to finish the job when I pulled him out of the house to attend services. Once in our new pew, he straddles me—I thought he was trying to climb over me—then brings his right knee down into my groin, a kind of Pop Warner Atomic Knee Drop. I hadn't read his anger, so the attack takes me by surprise. I am so mad, and in so much pain—the localized ball-fire morphing into a kind of hot-coals ache spreading through my lower abdomen—that I ask Laura for the car keys. I am close to bailing on church.

Instead I honor the anger, nodding offhandedly to my perfectly reasonable desire to gangster-slap my six-year-old. You are free to stay or leave, I say to the ugly red bolus of spite, but I will be moving on with my day . . . as soon as this fire in my nether regions goes out.

We head home after the insipid recessional hymn. (If slow, dirgelike, and obscure songs float your boat, St. Anselm's in Ross, California, is the parish for you.) I unload the dishwasher, clean the kitchen, write a sweet card to Laura—"I appreciate you now more than ever," blah blah blah—then drop off the dog for grooming. Today's marquee event is a birthday party at China Camp State Park for my buddy Gordon's two sons, Will and Griffin. I buy gifts on the way to the party, wrapping them in the store's parking lot, on the hood of the car, with paper, scissors, and tape I now keep in the back of the vehicle. Once at the park, we are warmly greeted by a host of familiar, smiling faces. Also present is Laura, who's come from the farmers' market in a separate car and asks me straightaway, "Did you put sunscreen on them?"

I have not. I had a lot of things going on, I explain, angling for forgiveness, understanding, maybe even a dollop of praise. "But you forgot the most important thing," she says, and I regret, for the briefest of moments, that it is too late to temper some of the sweetness in that card.

The party is a blast. Gordon and Ginny had the brilliant idea to give out, as favors, balsa airplanes with rubber-band propellers. Even the adults get into it. Soon there is a "boneyard" of broken planes, from which one can scavenge spare parts like whole tail sections and unruptured rubber bands. Several times, errant planes descend into a party of turbaned Muslims picnicking nearby. They endure the crash landings with stoicism.

With Operation Iraqi Freedom on everyone's mind, it is only a matter of time before someone cracks a joke. "Our balsa drones have unnerved them," observes Gordon. "They cannot escape our superior airpower."

We leave early. Laura is under the weather. She is also resentful, I have begun to suspect, of the kudos I am raking in for my triumphant debut on the local airwaves.

HAVING SPENT A LIFETIME PREPARING FOR FAME, I WAS NOT SUR-prised when Wayne Freedman, a reporter for KGO, San Francisco's ABC affiliate, gave me a call. Wayne's daughter is a close friend of Willa's. Having learned of the Experiment, he asked me if he and a cameraman could follow me around for a day.

While I pretended to have reservations, my only genuine concern was that my face would appear overly full, as it does when I've been eating too much ice cream. After getting clearance from the assistant principal, Wayne accompanied me into Devin's class for my Monday volunteer duties. This earned me cocked eyebrows from Lori F. and Donna G., a pair of moms who volunteer at the same time. (When I walked in the following week, Donna looked up from the folder she was stuffing and remarked, offhandedly, "What, no TV crew today, Austin?")

At home, while the camera rolled, I made a SpongeBob SquarePants sponge cake from a recipe in Willa's *Nickelodeon* magazine. (Ran into trouble where the recipe said, "Ask an adult to help you separate the egg whites and yolks"—Laura wasn't around.) I shared with Wayne a recent epiphany: I'd learned how to fold a fitted sheet. The cameraman sat in the passenger seat while I drove to school to pick the kids up. I pulled into the circle at upper as Deborah C. was pulling out. I believe I saw her jaw drop. It seemed to surprise her that I would be sharing the front seat of my car with a man who was training a bright light and an enormous TV camera on me.

On the phone with Deborah the next day, I explained what was going on. They're doing a short feature on me, to run on Mother's Day weekend!

It is a measure of our friendship that Deborah felt she could be honest with me. "I've been doing this for what feels like half my life," she said, "and of course it's incredibly fulfilling. Caring for and raising Jack and Anna is the most important work I could think of doing. That said, I've been doing it for nine years, and there are times when it feels like I'm invisible, that what I'm doing doesn't matter. You're in, what, you're fourth month? And you've got a television crew following you around."

That was eye-opening. "When I look at it from your perspective," I told Deborah, "I'm actually a little embarrassed." But not as embarrassed as I'll feel if the camera makes my face look puffy, like Renée Zellweger in one of those roles she has to pork up for.

Deborah's riff was my latest reminder that while I may be

trying to do hers and Laura's and millions of other women's jobs for half a year, I'm still no more than a day-tripper, an actor immersing himself in a role. *I'm not a real mother, but I play one on TV.* Laura makes this distinction between my experience and that of a real mom: "Real moms are going through their days and thinking, 'This is my life for the next twenty years.' You're thinking to yourself, 'All I need to do is hang on for three more months.'"

Striving for analogies, she decides that it is the difference between living together and being married; between doing Alcatraz as a tourist and actually marking time on the Rock.

I'm more committed to my job than that, although there are times when I find myself looking forward to the fall, to hearing the snick of the lock as the hotel room door closes behind me and knowing that, for at least a few hours, I am alone and accountable to no one.

DEVIN RETURNS FROM CHINA CAMP WITH A CRAB IN A PAPER CUP. not quite the size of a quarter, the critter scoots across D.'s palm. "His name is Clampy," Devin reports, "'cause he keeps trying to clamp my thumb with his pinchers."

Making it more difficult for Devin to bond with his new pet is Willa, who lectures him on the distressingly high number of endangered species in the world, including some crabs. "You realize by taking him home with you, he's going to die," she points out.

Devin denies that Clampy is doomed. "I'm going to keep him in my room," he vows.

"Okay, pop quiz," said Willa, who must be picking up this snarkiness at school. "You took him out of San Francisco Bay.

What kind of water comes out of our faucets, salt water or fresh water?"

Devin deftly avoids the trap. "I'll put salt in the fresh water," he promises.

Even though D. is good to his word, stirring table salt into Clampy's cup, the tiny crustacean loses vigor over the course of the afternoon, and has lapsed into a permanent napping state by dinnertime.

Willa can't resist a few I-told-you-so's. "I told you before we left that park he'd never make it, and now an innocent crab is dead because of you."

"I put some of Mommy's rice in the water," D. points out, in his defense. "But I can't communicate with crabs, so I couldn't tell him it was food. And he didn't know."

After reading time, I enter Devin's room to say good night. He is sniffling, and I see shiny little paths down his cheeks. "Do you have a cold?" I ask. "Or are you a little sad?"

"I have a cold *and* I'm sad" comes the reply. So I lie down and talk with him about how perfectly normal it is for boys to catch crabs and crawfish and lizards. I assure him I could tell that Clampy had enjoyed their brief friendship. I ask where Clampy is.

"In my treasure box," says D. "I wrapped him in a tissue." For one night, Clampy reposes on Devin's dresser. The following morning . . . well, by the following morning Clampy has been forgotten, and won't cross our minds for a good five days, by which time Laura and I will be wondering, *What's that smell coming from the back of the house?*

I AM CHILLING IN THE OFFICE AT LOWER CAMPUS THE NEXT MORN-ing, waiting to be noticed, having just deposited a plate of baked brown fragments in the teachers' lounge, in honor of Teacher Appreciation Week. (Dropping brownies off for the staff is not something you want to do *unobserved*.) Assistant Principal Finnane sees me and asks, "Did you get any Mother's Day cards?"

The fact is, I tell him, I got no love a tall. You'd think that just as a joke, someone would've acknowledged my servitude, maybe cut me some slack, lightened my load, given me a card. But no.

I never bring it up with Laura, but my guess is that this was her way of letting me know I hadn't *earned* a Mother's Day card. It was her way of saying, *You may have some TV reporter fooled; you may have deceived some of our friends and people in the community, but when it's just us, we both know that I'm still the sheriff in this house, still the authority figure who remembers sunscreen and doesn't leave the kids unattended in hotel rooms. To make some sort of fuss out of you on Mother's Day would be to reward you for a level of competence you haven't achieved.*

Fair enough. I still have work to do, miles to go before I sleep. I am erratic with the sunscreen, late with the bills, and still haven't signed the kids up for summer camp. But I'm doing a lot of things right, too.

Having helped my son cope with his bereavement last night, for instance, I cleaned the kitchen—Laura was already in bed, not feeling well—made lunches, then baked the dessert I would come to call "O.J.'s Alibi Brownies," because they crumbled at a touch. "Don't worry," I was assured by Marilyn, Mr. Finnane's assistant. "If they contain chocolate, they'll get eaten."

They didn't.

Before drifting off tonight, I reflect on yesterday's TV appearance, and smile the smile of one whose face did not appear bloated, after all; one whose labors were appreciated, if only by a few. At the end of the segment—this was actually my favorite part—the talent did that bantering-anchor thing.

"He's going to go back a better man," sighed Jessica Aguirre. She was talking about me.

"Or a beaten man," said Dan Ashley, her coanchor.

"That *is* a better man," Jessica insisted.

"Happy Mother's Day to all you real mothers out there," Dan continued. "And to you too, Austin. You're doing a good job."

Thanks, Dan. It was nice of you to notice.

The Longest Week

Even though she despises the sport, cannot see the fun in it, and resents the time it takes me away from home, Laura has given me permission to do an adventure race.

I used to do triathlons. But you get tired, after a while, of being around a bunch of unsmiling cyborgs who'd rather study their heart-rate monitors than return your friendly greeting, who are blind to the fact that there is something more than a little strange about hordes of adult men with shaved legs and taped nipples running through neighborhoods in Speedos.

What I like most about adventure racing is the team dynamic. When a teammate is hurting, you offer to lighten his load, secure in the knowledge that when you're having a low moment, he'll be there for you. Also, people don't tend to shave their legs for this sport.

My buddy Gordon and I have been doing adventure races for a few years. Having graduated from half-day races to twenty-four-hour events, we felt we were ready to take the next step. So a year ago, we showed up at the starting line of the Appalachian Extreme, a 256-mile race in western Maine.

My biggest concern going into that race was our fitness. It's hard to properly train for one of these beasts when you're also attempting to hold down a job and at least go through the motions of being a good husband and father.

Fitness, it turned out, was the least of our problems.

In this sport, teams of between two and four people race over difficult terrain, night and day. Shortly before the event, competitors are given maps and a series of checkpoints. It is the team's job to plot those checkpoints on the map, then bag them in the prescribed order. There are trekking sections, paddling sections, mountain-biking sections. There are fixed ropes for ascending and rappelling. It doesn't matter how strong you are at any of those disciplines if you can't navigate.

We couldn't navigate our way out of a paper bag. Team Marin—that was Gordon, me, and our erratic navigator—was lost early and often. We stunk, and we stunk.

For a day and a night we were a middle-of-the-pack team. That was as good as it got. Having misplotted Checkpoint 14, we spent our second night trudging through a bog, encountering innumerable moose pies but no checkpoint. On the third morning of the race, forty-one hours into a trekking section that had taken the lead teams fourteen hours to complete, we busted out our emergency radio and quit.

Race director Tracyn Thayer was somewhat relieved to hear from us. She'd just called the Maine State Police to initiate a search and rescue. Back at race headquarters, we'd been nick-named "Team Moron."

"You might want to think about sticking around for the party," she told us Morons as we glumly packed our bags. "You know—to defend yourselves."

We didn't stick around.

LAURA HAD INFORMED ME, UPON OUR RETURN TO CALIFORNIA, that additional adventure races would cost me money.

"How much," I said.

"Three thousand dollars," she replied.

"Why three thousand dollars?"

"That's about how much it would cost me to stay a week at Rancho La Puerta."

I couldn't really argue. She was right: I spent so much time traveling for my job, it was selfish to take additional time away from our nuclear family just to cop some adrenaline rush. But early in my tenure as Mr. Mom, she'd given me a very generous gift. "Because you are giving me all this time," she'd said, "I will waive my fee for this year's race." She'd made it very clear that this was a one-year exemption.

So, on the weekend before Memorial Day, we show up again at the Appalachian Extreme, hoping to redeem ourselves. This year we've got a new name—Team King Oscar, for the Norway-based sardine colossus whose publicity on this continent is so ably managed by Gordon—and a new navigator. His name is Eddie Freyer. Eddie has done two Eco-Challenges and is way over our heads. He says he will race with us because we make him laugh. We're not sure how to take that, but we're glad to have him.

You can't do one of these races without a support crew. For the second year in a row, we've roped in my brother Mark, who lives outside Portland, Maine; and my sister Gibby and her husband, John, up from Virginia. This is the same trio that sat around for waiting for us for forty-one hours last year, so you can't blame them for expecting very little from us in '03. After we breeze through check-in, providing proof of health insurance and showing race officials our mandatory gear, Mark deadpans, "You might want to get their dental records, too."

It is my brother-in-law who notes that the beauty of the first section, a forty-seven-mile paddle on the Connecticut, is that "even you guys can't get lost on a river." Nor do we. We come out of the water sixth from last. (Note to self: next year, maybe spend more than a total of ninety minutes training for the paddling sections.) Then we jump on our bikes and start picking off teams.

By the time we pedal into the sixth checkpoint, we can tell that Eddie isn't himself. Our first clue: we've been able to keep up with him. After putting away a Coke and a bowl of chili, he shuffles weakly to a spot behind the team truck and vomits with such gusto, according to Mark, that "it didn't even touch his teeth."

Eddie ralphs twice more over the next hour before enduring— *Injury, have you met Insult?*—an urgent bout of diarrhea. He is in a sleeping bag as one of the physicians working the race explains, in comforting tones, the upside of an antinausea injection. "Whatever," says Eddie, then drops trou and takes one for the team. A nanosecond after the needle goes in, he turns as white as Wednesday Addams and emits an eerie moan. It scares the shit out of us. His eyes roll up in his head, his body jerks in a brief spasm—a certain sardine flack among us insists on calling it a seizure—and he passes out.

Seizure or not, Eddie is having a rough night.

The nurse who administered the shot recognizes the episode as a "vasovagal faint." People who are freaked out by needles (as Eddie is, he later admits) sometimes swoon right after they get a shot. When Eddie comes to, ten or so seconds later, he finds himself gazing up at a circle of concerned faces and thinking, he will later recall, *Where am I?*

While Eddie groans through a night of fitful sleep, Team King Oscar settles comfortably into last place, eight hours behind the next-worst team. Our navigator is a pale, dehydrated shell of himself. Our race is probably over.

Or is it? At dawn, Eddie rises from his sleeping bag, takes a few uncertain steps, burps ominously, and says, "Might as well give it a try."

I thank Eddie then, thank him throughout the next two days, and am thanking him now for having had the courage to keep going. As the morning wears on, and he is able to hold down a bit of food—energy gels, sports drinks, Gibby's patented gorp— he picks up his pace. For a profanity-eliciting, uphill, two-mile bushwhack over crosshatched deadfall of birch and pine, our reward is Checkpoint 8, atop thirty-five-hundred-foot Percy Peak. Lovelier than the White Mountains arrayed before us is the realization that Eddie is on the mend.

At checkpoint 10 we are told that we have passed a team that's been out all night searching for Percy Peak. We're thrilled to no longer occupy last place. Let's face it: schadenfreude is as much a part of this sport as blisters and trekking poles. By the time we glissade down the loose gravel from Dixville Peak and hit checkpoint 15, we've been out for sixteen hours and put five more teams behind us.

During the dastardly forty-mile mountain bike that follows, we pass another six squads, including Team Workhorse, a trio of gimlet-eyed army officers who spend eight hours looking for checkpoint 16, then run up the white flag.

After twenty fast miles of biking on paved roads to Gorham, New Hampshire, we board canoes for the chilly, nocturnal, twenty-four-mile paddle down the Androscoggin River back to Bethel, Maine.

Where we finish—eleventh out of twenty-five teams—is less important to us than the fact that we finish, period. It feels good to redeem ourselves, to cross the line and hug everyone in sight. If feels good to eat pizza at five in the morning, then fall asleep in the bathtub with a bottle of beer. It feels good, walking into that party.

I GET US UPGRADES FOR THE FLIGHTS HOME. GORDON ALMOST certainly will get around to thanking me, but the trip only takes eight hours. Once we have some beers in front of us, it is time to initiate our postrace You Scratch My Back ritual, in which one team member lavishes compliments on the other, with the understanding that this flattery will quickly be reciprocated. For instance:

"Murph, I can't believe you got halfway down the Connecticut with that crappy paddle. That was nails."

"No—when you cleaned that nasty section of fire road on the way up CP Eighteen—*that* was nails."

"Had to, bro. You were right on my tail."

And so on, until we drift off, or the flight lands.

One of the many questions we ask, in recounting every detail of our triumph, is: Which day was hardest? Was it Day 1, with the monster paddle? Or Day 3, with all that hike-a-biking and tricky nav?

I have no idea, flying home from the Appalachian Extreme, that the toughest day of my week lies not behind me but ahead.

ON THE CALENDAR, IT LOOKED LIKE A RELAXING IDYLL. WE ARE headed south, on this Memorial Day weekend, to Big Basin Redwoods State Park. There, with Deborah and Paul and their children, Anna and Jack, we will commune with the majestic redwoods, will decompress, will slow the pace of our lives.

That's the plan, at any rate.

That first night, with the children zipped into their sleeping bags and kissed good night, the adults stay up around the fire, unburdening ourselves of our cares. Deborah's got a big tap recital next week. As if that isn't stressful enough, the choreographer put her right next to the statuesque blond who is far and away the best tapper in the class. She is concerned she may suffer by comparison. I ask if the words "Tonya Harding" mean anything to her.

Paul's got his own problems. He works for Pixar, and has been up to his eyeballs these last few months tying up loose ends for the picture they're about to release—some cartoon whose main characters are a pair of clown fish. Between you and me, I can't see this thing doing much box office.

I'm concerned that if I have a third glass of wine, I might have to leave the tent in the middle of the night to take a leak. I pour myself a stiff one anyway, raising my glass to the end of a long day.

Did I say a long day? Make that longer than long. Make that the longest day of my life, with the possible exception of the day of the Big Snip. Next to the sustained, grueling servitude of May 24 the adventure race was penny-ante stuff. I'm serious. With Eddie on the compass and our crack support crew forcing food on us during breaks, all I had to do during the adventure race was suffer physically.

Today's torments were multidimensional—mental and physical. I do the mom stuff—the packing, planning, and logistics—*and* the dad stuff—hauling, driving, setting up camp. This, of course, is Laura's lot when a camping trip is planned but work calls me away at the last minute, as has happened several times. "And that is why," she tells me, after listening to me bitch for a spell, "I generally loathe camping." I'm seeing things her way while ticking items off a Saturday to-do list that goes something like this:

Plan menus for three days, shop for food, pack for the kids, pack for self (Laura selflessly volunteers to do her own packing), drive to Gordon's to borrow needed gear, pack car (a task made more challenging by the need to bring Laura's six-inch foam sleeping pad), do MapQuest search, get out of car to ask directions when MapQuest directions prove worse than useless, stand in fifteen-minute line to secure campsite from harried, humorless ranger in order to return to the car—in which spouse has remained—to be asked: Did you remember to get some good hiking suggestions?

Unpack car (seven trips ferrying gear four hundred yards uphill to campsite), repark car a mile away in overflow lot, gallantly allowing late-arriving friends to take the single spot allotted to our campsite. Hike back from overflow lot with kids, who view this exertion as a forced march and Geneva Convention violation. Assist in unpacking friends' truck—five trips (but who's counting?) for coolers, equipment boxes, and, finally, firewood—while friend stands in campsite chatting up my wife. Pitch tent. Finish pitching second tent, on which wife and daughter had begun work before abandoning. Cook, then serve dinner. Scrape, wash pots, dishes, silver. Dry same.

Realize, during KP duty, that I've spent half the day in our outdoor "cathedral" without yet experiencing any decompression whatsoever.

All the work was worth it, of course, when the campfire was lit and the marshmallows came out. That's right, kids: it's s'mores time—the highlight of any camping trip!

I wish I were serious. I wish I liked s'mores, because it makes me feel Scrooge-like and mean-spirited when I inveigh against them. But seriously, this has to be the most overrated dessert in history.

To those readers who have recently emigrated from Madagascar, a s'more consists of a roasted marshmallow atop a small sheet of chocolate, pressed viselike between two squares of graham cracker. In theory, the molten mallow melts the chocolate, fusing the three components into a single, delectable treat.

Except that, in recorded history, the marshmallow has never actually melted the chocolate, ensuring that the s'more fractures upon the first bite, sending an avalanche of chocolate and cracker to earth and providing the child/victim an excuse to cry for still another s'more.

Paul and Deborah, who own roughly twice as much camping equipment we do, had brought along a pair of telescoping marshmallow rods. Which meant that at least two children were without the roasting apparati, ensuring a constant level of high-pitched whining and recriminations.

Kids know in their heart of hearts that s'mores are overrated. They have taste buds. It's just that they're willing to overlook this shortcoming because s'mores are the only dessert in history absolutely requiring them to play with fire.

After we had walked the quarter mile to the restrooms and supervised tinkling and toothbrushing and the sandblasting of hardened marshmallow from freckled faces; after the little ones had changed their minds ten or so times on sleeping configurations—boys and girls would be in separate tents; Devin would sleep with Mom and Dad, Jack with the girls; no, they would all sleep together—they finally decide on the last arrangement, and conk out immediately . . . after eleven P.M.

Damn straight I had that third glass of vino.

It is decided on Sunday morning that the children will do the dishes—let them start to pull some of their weight around here!—but this is a fiasco. Arguing over which of them will man the spigot of the fountain near our site, Devin and Jack create a good-sized wetland for migrating waterfowl, but clean no dishes. Banishing them, I take over. The girls are on drying duty. Anna dries a fork or plate, then tosses it toward a nearby tray, which she hits about a third of the time, ensuring that most of the just-washed utensils come to rest in the dirt, which sticks, as Anna—an otherwise charming and talented child—is an indifferent dryer. After ten minutes of this I thank Anna and Willa for their assistance and send them away as well.

Around the fire the night before, Deborah had talked about the importance of giving the children jobs and allowing them to finish—even if you could do that job faster yourself. "Otherwise," she said, "you're perpetuating your own enslavement."

So, in addition to choosing a route for our hike this morning, I am perpetuating my own enslavement. That's how Deborah sees it. The truth, of course, is that Laura and I will be trading back in a few months, and I will go out on the road again for long stretches. So it is her enslavement I am perpetuating.

If it means getting to the bottom of this pile of pots any faster, I'm okay with that.

I sleep more deeply on this second night in the wild—until Willa comes whimpering to the tent at 3:45 A.M., the blackest minute of the darkest hour of night. Unlike her mother, who doesn't like to stray, say, more than four feet from the tent before cutting loose with her nocturnal whiz—who knows what's out there?—Princess Willa would never consider making water outdoors. Groping blindly for flashlight, then sandals, I walk with her to the lavatory. It's the least I can do.

Laura cannot stop exulting in the morning about what great sleep she's getting, on her foam mattress, with her fleece eye mask, but none of the rest of us really want to hear it. We're shuffling around, bleary-eyed, halitosis-afflicted, presenting children with food and drink while waiting for the water to boil, so we can make coffee.

I am given the job of sunscreen application—getting a nose ring in a wild boar would be no more difficult—for our upcoming hike, a mile of which I will spend carrying my nearly eighty-pound son. After breaking down the camp, I lug the heavy things to the car. Upon completing the two-hour drive home, I transition seamlessly from Camp Bee-atch to House Bee-atch, unloading the car, getting dinner on the table, getting the children unpacked, making their lunches for school tomorrow.

It is during this final exercise that my thoughts drift to Team King Oscar's final hours on the Androscoggin, six nights earlier. After biking to Gorham, New Hampshire, we'd boarded canoes in darkness, then embarked on that long, bone-chilling paddle to the finish. That leg of the race featured three pain-in-the-ass portages, hypothermia, and hallucinations. So badly did I want to see man-made structures that, after four hours in the boat, I began to imagine them.

It's warm in the kitchen, I have to admit, slicing apples that are all but sure to go uneaten. But at least in Maine there was a goddam finish line.

As Good As It Gets

The End-of-the-Year Slide is upon us. That is the name bestowed on these final few weeks of school by veteran Brookside parents and teachers. The Slide is characterized by the smorgasbord of events—music demonstrations, field trips postponed by weather, class parties, the Parents Club Social—that end up being scheduled in the final weeks of school.

Add to that calendar clutter this newly minted perennial, the Lower Brookside Variety Show. For this, we can all thank Assistant Principal David Finnane, a man with a tremendous deal of pride in his school, yet not so much pride—this is often true of visionaries—that he has any qualms about delegating responsibility and dreaming up work for others.

I'd explained to David in mid-February that I was a sportswriter on sabbatical. I'd told him to keep me in mind for any volunteer work. After learning that I covered college football, then wearing me out for ten minutes on why 2003 would probably be a breakout year for the Wisconsin Badgers (they would lose, at home, to UNLV in September), he told me he might have something for me sooner rather than later. A week or so later, I had a new title, of which I was sufficiently proud to mention it on my answering machine:

You've reached Austin Murphy, chairman of the Lower Brookside Variety Show. Please feel free to leave a message for the chairman at the beep.

Finnane's sister's kids go to a school in East Grand Rapids, Michigan, that is renowned for its butt-kicking talent shows. Not that he's at all competitive, but this got the wheels turning beneath David's ruggedly handsome pate. Why shouldn't his fiefdom, lower campus, have its own talent show? He gave me a phone number and these instructions: "Give this guy a call."

ABOUT THIRTY SECONDS INTO MY TWENTY-MINUTE CONVERSATION with Eric, who has organized two dozen talent shows at the Wealthy Elementary School—its actual name—in East Grand Rapids, I can tell that our humble revue will not be up to Wealthy standards. He is going on about their use of high-tech Elmo analog presenters, speaking excitedly of how their students project video and computer-generated images onto screens behind the performers. "You wouldn't have to be that elaborate," he says.

"I would think we'd want to be as, or more, elaborate," I say, while thinking, *Does our stage even have a curtain?*

He does give me some advice we can apply directly to our

show. We will want to announce a kickoff meeting for all inter-ested parties. We'll also need a theme. Down through the years at the Wealthy Elementary, themes have ranged from "Fiesta" to "Circus" to "Space" to "Mister Rogers' Neighborhood"— although those last two are probably out of consideration, owing to the sad, recent demise of both the space shuttle *Columbia* and the Man in the Cardigan.

I present my findings at the first meeting of the Lower Brook-side Variety Show Committee, attended by four teachers—Tri-cia M., Anne M., Katrine H., Jennifer H.—myself, David, school psychologist Erin J., and librarian Cori K. After listening raptly to all I have to say, they quickly conclude:

A. We don't need no stinking theme.
B. We don't need no stinking kickoff meeting.

I am reminded that the parents of our students are stretched thin as it is; the students themselves are ludicrously over-scheduled. The last thing they need in their lives is another mandatory meeting.

We decide instead to send out a memo announcing the date and location of the show (June 6 in the upper campus auditorium) and describing what we are looking for: a variety of acts, from lip-synchers, instrumentalists, and poem readers to Elvis impersonators. Involvement will entail an audition and rehearsals.

"I could write that letter and whip up some kind of contract," I volunteer.

"Why else do you think you're here?" says Finnane, and he

and the members of his staff have a good laugh at my expense. "I need it by Friday."

Part of David's administrative genius, of course, is his ability to know which buttons to push to get the best results from his minions. He has somehow intuited that this is the sort of brusque leadership to which I respond.

The memos and contracts go home with the bulletins in the kids' backpacks. We aren't expecting much of a response. The Wealthy School is kindergarten through fifth grade. Here at lower, we go K through second. I have serious doubts that we'll get more than a dozen acts.

We get forty-one.

We split up into three groups and spend a week of lunch periods reviewing the acts. Some are ready for prime time. Lauren E.'s frenetic Avril Lavigne impersonation, complete with necktie, kicks ass, as does Fiona S.'s Irish step dancing and tiny Sarah M.'s rendition of "Over the Rainbow." Others need work.

A lot of work. Mostly, the acts run long. Taylor W.'s basketball clinic, presented with his buddy Cayman B., goes over eight minutes. "Guys," I tell them, "if everyone takes eight minutes, people in the audience will need sleeping bags."

I'm worried about my buddy Sean B., a second grader with cerebral palsy. This kid is a battler and an inspiration, locomoting around lower campus with the help of a walker, picking himself up when he takes a spill, always grinning, his great big eyes magnified through the thick lenses of his Harry Potter frames. The school district has provided him with a one-on-one aide, Eric L., a friendly, athletic-looking guy just out of college who is seldom far from his side. Eric and I hang out a little when I'm on campus. I slide him an extra slice or two when I fill in on pizza day. I like the way he works with Sean, getting the kid into the mix of things on the playground. Sean even plays kickball. He takes an at-bat, and the other kids are cool with him having a pinch runner.

Sean has heard about the Variety Show, and he wants in. This kid leads with his chin. On the day of his scheduled rehearsal, he and Eric show up in the computer room, next to the library. Eric tells us Sean is going to tell a few jokes, then sing a song.

But the little guy speaks so softly while telling the jokes that it's hard to hear him. He loses his way telling his first knock-knock joke, then gets a little turned around—and who among us hasn't?—navigating his way through "Do Re Mi." To get him through it, we all take up the chorus—me, Finnane, Eric, and a couple of teachers. It's kind of a sweet moment. Our smiles at the end of the song can't disguise the fact that this has been a less than auspicious debut for the lad. I emphasize to Eric that he and Sean need to make sure they've got their act together by showtime.

We have another meeting ten days before the show. I need to get the program typed up. I need to make sure we have a proper sound system in the auditorium. I need to call the parents of the kids whose acts still stink after two rehearsals, just to make sure they are on the case. Also, since Mr. Finnane, school psychologist Erin J., and I are emcees, David wonders if it wouldn't be too much trouble for me to hit a few costume shops around town. He thoughtfully provides me with his measurements.

Once the man gets some momentum—this is often the case with talented adminstrators—he can easily find himself on a delegating roll. "Wouldn't it be great," he goes on, "if we could get a few kids on stilts outside the auditorium on the day of the show? And someone on a unicycle!" (The muse is on him now.)

He throws out the name of a Brookside mom whose middle school-aged son rides a unicycle. Could someone get on that?

Three days before the show I pull into the parking lot at lower campus and there he is, shouting at me from the window of his Jeep: "We've got T minus seventy-two hours—I should be talking to you three, four times a day."

I haven't noticed my phone ringing off the hook, I tell him. The truth is, if I call the guy, he'll give me five more jobs. I'm in so far over my head already, so acutely aware of the excellent odds that something will go badly wrong, that I'm already resigned to a gong show, a free-for-all, a chocolate mess.

The next day I have messages from several moms, asking me to move the time of their kids' acts, plus a message from Der Kommissar, suggesting that in my free time I alert the *Ross Valley Reporter* and the *Marin Independent Journal*.

Yeah, David, I think, *I'll get right on that.*

I SHOW UP AT THE AUDITORIUM EARLY ON THE MORNING OF THE show. I've arranged the CDs and cassettes—thirty in all—in the order in which they'll be played. It only took me till midnight to get that straightened out. Before long, kids are pouring into the place, and it's time for Finnane and me to change into our outfits, rented from D'Lynnes's, a great costume store I found in San Rafael. He's wearing a lime-green suit complete with a phat top hat; if a pimp ever appeared in a work by Lewis Carroll, this is what he would look like. I'm in a red velour, puffy-sleeved Austin Powers getup, complete with black frames. "Oh, behave," I will repeat, intermittently, for the next four hours. Cohost No. 3, Erin J., is a bit late emerging from the changing room. Erin, one of your more voluptuous school psychologists, hadn't had time to try on the skintight, silver lamé Cher outfit we picked out for her. The ensemble turns out to be a tad revealing, requiring Cher to spend a quarter hour or so in the changing room with a roll of duct tape. When she emerges, all the hatches are battened down, and we can proceed.

The kids are slow to simmer down, and we're seven minutes late getting started. Not good. Excluding a forty-five-minute lunch break, we'll have two hours to knock out forty-one performances. Our first act, the Abba Dancers, is high-energy and polished, by the standards of our show, but their medley does go a little long. We have curtain issues with the trio of mimes that follow. Erin is announcing their act when the fourth graders in charge of the curtain close it on her. We give these kids one job and they screw it up.

We're still working the bugs out when Sean B. makes his appearance on stage. He's forgone his walker and crash helmet for the occasion, choosing to simply hold on tight to the hand of Eric, who puts the mike next to Sean's mouth. There is a pause, then a longer pause, and then silence. Finally Sean introduces himself. He is barely audible. Oh boy.

"And I'm his buddy Eric," says Eric. "We're gonna tell a couple jokes, then sing a song."

He puts the mike back in front of Sean, a wiry little guy who seems especially small up there, except for those eyes.

"A joke," he whispers. Then, as if remembering why he is up there, he says, "Joke number one, coming up."

Feeding on the trickle of laughs that line gets, Sean speaks slightly louder: "Knock, knock," he says, and the entire auditorium shouts back, "WHO'S THERE?"

"Boo."

"BOO WHO?"

"Don't cry." Except with his lisp it comes out "Don't cwy." There is as much relief as amusement, I think, in the laughter that follows.

Another knock-knock joke—"Tennis." "TENNIS WHO?" "Tennis more than nine."—is followed by "joke number three," my personal favorite:

"Why don't lions eat clams?"

"WHY?"

"Because they taste funny."

Having warmed up the crowd, the eight-year-old makes ready to sing. All I can think, as he stands in front of half a thousand people, is that he struggled in rehearsal. I sit in the wings fearing the worst.

As with his foray into stand-up comedy, Sean starts slowly, and it will occur to me afterward that the kid might have been sandbagging us, lowering our expectations so he could blow us away:

Do, a deew, a female deew—the lisp slays me—

Way, a dwop of golden sun,

Me, a name I CALL MYSELF—his voice swelling on those last three syllables; he is gaining confidence—

Fa, a long long way to run.

So, a needle pulling thwead,

La, a note to follow SO-oo-oo—someone in the audience cuts loose with a "Whoooo!"

Tea, a dwink of jam and bwead—of jam, with jam, whatever!

That will bwing us . . . back . . . to . . .

But his last, Homer Simpsonesque *Doh!* is drowned out by a torrent of applause from his fellow students, and from the two hundred or so parents arrayed around the auditorium, many of whom are moist-eyed by the time he finishes. Sean and Eric bow from the waist, as one, and cheers wash over them.

His mother, Eri, tells me later that Sean loves to sing, which makes sense. He can't always get his body to cooperate with his mind, but he can hold a tune. Months later, after I've gone back to my real job, it will occur to me how prone we sportswriters are to overusing the word *courage*. Bob Stoops calls a fake punt from his own thirty-one-yard line at Alabama? Josh Beckett takes the mound against the Yankees on three days' rest? Give these men Bronze Stars for valor!

What Sean has done, walking out in front of five hundred people on legs that don't cooperate with his brain—that took stainless steel cojones. (When you're old enough, Sean, your dad can tell you what those are.)

Even though the show is still young after Sean's performance, I cannot help but decompress. A sense of well-being, an assurance that, somehow, everything will be okay, comes over me. For once it is not a portent of disaster.

Cayman and Taylor, the guys who showed up at rehearsal with a basketball clinic that ran as long as the *Oresteia,* turn in a brisk, Cliffs Notes version of their first performance. Even with some material I might have edited out—*Now I will show you the left-hand dribble, which is just like the right-hand dribble, except with the left hand*—they come in around three minutes. Great job, guys.

We cruise the rest of the way. When Jan Bishop can't find the music for the juggling act after the intermezzo, I take the stage and fill. "We were going to have a spotlight," I explain, "but the glare off Mr. Finnane's head was making it tough for some of the kids to read their poems."

Before it can be over, we must abide the sight of the faculty, dressed in "Western" wear, performing a line dance. I've spent a month making sure the kids keep their the acts close to two minutes. Here are their teachers now, taking four-plus. And because of the music they chose—the widely dreaded "Electric Slide"—it seems like ten.

At long last, it is over. There follows a quarter hour of chatter on the floor of the auditorium that may strike some as banal and of little consequence, but I recall it as a scene of triumph.

In those sweet moments, in the golden penumbra that does not actually exist in the auditorium but which my memory will soon provide, I am approached by half a dozen women whose work I admire. Moms whose standards I aspire to now look me in the eye and tell me, "Great job." Their praise is ambrosia to me. It intoxicates.

In the remaining months of my Mr. Mom–hood I will foul up, fall on my face, and piss down my leg, as usual. It will take me three separate trips to the grocery store to get the proper-sized garbage bag for our kitchen wastebasket. I will repeatedly pick up the high-end toilet paper with about three dozen "squares" per roll, which lasts half a day in a house whose occupants include a boy who insists on performing what he calls "the Superwipe." (Don't ask.)

In bringing off the Variety Show, however, I have taken a giant step forward, made a statement. I have played the game at a high level, have earned the praise and respect of a tough crowd. When he is challenged by the impertinent young Nuke LaLoosh in *Bull Durham,* Kevin Costner's journeyman catcher, Crash Davis, responds wistfully, "Yeah, I was in the Show. I was in the Show for twenty-one days once—the best twenty-one days of my life."

The Variety Show is my cup of coffee in the Show, my one-afternoon to stand shoulder to shoulder with the Brookside moms, some of the best in the world at what they do. For this brief, shining moment, I feel like a pro.

The problem with this accursed gig is that you never pop the champagne, spray your teammates, then allow yourself to be pulled away to field a few questions from Tim McCarver. In keeping with the rules of the game, the job is not finished. There are folding chairs to be stacked, and there is tape to be pulled up, wadded into balls, and flung at Devin, flung toward distant trash receptacles, and flung at the preposterous top hat sported by Mr. Finnane, who approaches me, now that the crowd has dispersed, with his hand outstretched.

I know what comes next. This is where he dispenses with the testosterone-induced posturing and tells me how none of this could've happened without me, where he flings open the window to his soul and thanks me from the bottom of his heart.

"Dude," he says, "can you do me a favor? I've gotta get back to the office. Could you drop my costume off for me?"

Bridge Week

You get into the writing business to feed your ego, to see your name and words in print. That it also happens to be spectacularly remunerative, that sportswriters, for whatever reason, attract some of the world's most beautiful women—these are added bonuses.

The money, the women—I'm joking about those things, obviously. But the ego part is true. Why else am I doing it? Because I can't get enough of the Texas State Fair? (The *farr,* as locals call it, is the backdrop for the annual Texas-Oklahoma game, which it appears to be my fate to be assigned to cover every October until I retire or am crushed beneath the wheels of the Sooner Schooner, whichever comes first.)

So it's been a slight adjustment, getting *SI* in the mail and seldom having a byline, wondering if they miss me at the magazine, if they've noticed that I'm gone. To fill the void and feed the ego, I've come up with byline substitutes. When Kandee, the principal, drops a note to thank me for my efforts on "upper campus landscaping day," that's a byline. When Finnane gives me a long-sleeved Wisconsin jersey for my Variety Show efforts, or when Nancy S. compliments the way I ran the soapstone-carving station during Miwok Day—"You made it fun to volunteer," she says, and I want to kiss her—those are bylines.

I cop my most prestigious byline on June 11. That's the day of Devin's "promotion ceremony" from kindergarten. I didn't get a promotion ceremony from kindergarten, and probably neither did you. But kindergarten is harder these days. These kids have busted their little tails, are counting to a hundred, and have mastered, in most cases, simple writing. Let's give it up for the little shits. On the morning of the ceremony, a few volunteer dads set up folding chairs out on the baseball field. Camcorders start whirring as the children promenade out. They have taken their seats facing us before Jan realizes they've left their sprigs of lavender in their cubbies. Back they go. Everyone takes the false start in stride but one type A dad, a guy with a commuter mug attached to his waistband, who says, "I've gotta be in Oakland at ten o'clock, so let's *go!*"

A few of the Power Mommies are called to the front. Jan hands them a gift and talks about their special contributions: "Erin B., you're my right and left hand, my guardian angel" . . . "Gina F., my friend and collaborator, always there to catch me when, for instance, I leave the lavender in the cubbies."

Then she calls my name, and I can't even hear what she says. There is applause, and a rush of blood to the head. I am presented with a purple cloth bag—ideal for bringing reading material to the beach, say, or for use as grocery tote at Good Earth, where its presence on the checkout counter will fairly shout to other parents: "That's right, I recycle, *and* I volunteer so extensively at my child's school that they gave me this handsome sack! What do you do?"

Imprinted on the bag is a lime-green butterfly, its wings made up of Devin's lime-green handprints. Beneath the butterfly, Jan has written, "Thanks for lending us a hand." All of this is in keeping with a school year–long theme. When their names are called, the kids walk to Jan, who presents them with construction-paper butterflies. Earlier in the year, the class had monitored the metamorphosis of a chrysalis into a monarch butterfly, which was then released, an occasion of great pomp. On this momentous morning, we reflect on the symbolism of the butterfly. "All of you," says Jan, "are ready to take wing." Slumped in his seat, mouth open, finger in his nose, fly halfway down, T-shirt not quite covering his gut, Devin doesn't appear to be a candidate to take wing, but I know what Jan means.

In the milling around afterward, I definitely notice a mom or two casting sidelong glances at my bag—I'm talking here about the tribute from Jan—moms who hadn't been singled out and may have been wondering, *What did he do that I didn't?* I have no time for such pettiness. By now, many of the children are presenting gifts to Jan. Readers who have made it this far will not be surprised to learn that I have purchased no such gift. "Devin," I say, "that's our cue to amscray."

It's the last day of school at upper campus, too. After gathering her third-grade class and their parents, Ruth Leader makes like the Wizard of Oz, dispensing certificates to each student, citing qualities they've exhibited during the school year:

"Stephen," she says, meaning Spiderboy, "accuracy and neatness" . . . "Nava, generosity and conservation" . . . "Mary-Margaret, persistence and dedication" . . . "Jessie, determination and perseverance." The fact that Ruth has to double-dip on some of the qualities—persistence and imagination crop up more than once—detracts not a whit from this very sweet ceremony. It is touching how much thought went into this.

Gloria B., who is not just our room parent but a *room parent's room parent,* in the sense that my younger brother Matt was not just a bouncer but a *bouncer's bouncer,* stands up and speaks from her heart, singing the praises of Mrs. Leader. Ruth, you will recall, spent the bulk of the school year working through the effects of chemo, yet showed up for class every morning bright-eyed and raring to impart knowledge. When she felt like crud, she came to school anyway, forced a smile on her face, and got through the day.

"You taught us parents, too," says Gloria, "about courage, and facing challenges and getting through them in the most amazing way. You are an incredible woman, and if you ever need a job, come over and organize my life."

The students, by then, have moved on to other things. Many are measuring themselves against the wall where they'd marked their height at the beginning of the year. After Gloria embraces Ruth, her daughter Amanda wanders past the parents, looks around, and remarks, "This is scary. All the grown-ups are crying."

Laden down though I am by the artwork and posterboard projects of my daughter the prodigy, the walk to the car is a social ramble. So many moms, so little time. There is Deborah, there is Catherine, there is Nancy. *What are your vacation plans? What camps are the kids signed up for? Call me. We'll set up a playdate.*

After my fourth or fifth such exchange, I make a move toward another mother—a lovely woman with a Jessica Rabbit figure and a tattoo much discussed by Brookside dads—but Willa clamps a death grip on my wrist. "Dad," she says, "are you going to stop and talk to *every mom you see?*"

That's the idea, pretty much, I would have said, had I been honest with her.

Not because I intend to flirt with them. I'm way past that with the Brookside moms. The truth is that over these past months, school has become the place I go to have conversations with adults other than my wife. On this, the last day of school, I mourn the loss of my social life.

LAURA IS GONE AGAIN, THIS TIME TO THE EAST COAST FOR ELEVEN days. She has sandwiched interviews with magazine editors around a long weekend in the Hamptons. Our friend Maura is turning forty.

I am on my own for Bridge Week, my name for the seven days between school's end and the glorious morning I pack their lunches, coat them with sunscreen, and deposit their chunky white asses at camp.

Camp. The very word mocks me. Three months earlier, I'd e-mailed Susan C. on the subject of camps. I know this, because she later took pleasure in forwarding me a copy of the note I sent. Susan's youngest son, Griffin, is one of Devin's school buddies. My e-mail to Susan said:

If Griffin's going to be doing any camps this summer, give me a heads-up. I'm looking at the San Anselmo spring rec. catalog now. The knowledge that G. might be at a certain camp would make it much easier to get slug-boy out the door in the morning.

We went back and forth, finally agreeing to sign our guys up for the second session of Millennium Madness, at the park across the street from my house.

Next thing you know, March is over, April showers have become May flowers, I'm hip-deep in the Variety Show, and I still haven't signed anyone up for camp. Finally, on June 7, I dropped by the offices of the town Rec Center. "I know it's late to get kids signed up for camp," I said, but the college-age kid behind the counter waved my worries aside. "We have plenty of openings," he said.

"Thank God," I said. "I need to get both my kids in Millennium Madness, Session Two." That was the session all their friends were already enrolled in, because the field trip was to— Water World!

"Except Session Two," said the guy, to whom I was taking more and more of a dislike. "That's the only one that's totally booked. I can put you on the waiting list."

They put me on a waiting list. Outside, the sun shone down brilliantly, but my world was overcast. What was it Laura had told me in February? *Smart working moms get their kids signed up for camp early.* With each footfall on the long, lugubrious walk home I heard her voice saying, "I told you so . . . I told you so . . . I told you so."

She'd told me so. Now I had to break the news to Susan C., who had, upon my urging, signed Griffin up for Millennium Madness with the expectation that his buddy would be there with him. On the morning of the promotion ceremony, I spilled my guts to Susan, admitting that I'd procrastinated and had gotten burned. A striking blond with a direct gaze, she never changed her expression while I spoke, or even after I'd finished, when she said through her smile, "I'm going to kill you."

It all worked out. She did not, in fact, execute me, deserving though I was. We signed both guys up for Canon Sports Camp—a superior camp but more expensive, and not walking distance from the house. (Willa was already registered to go there.) Unregistering Griffin from the camp I'd asked her to sign him up for wasn't a huge problem, or so she claimed.

I do a better job getting through Bridge Week than I did during Laura's four-day absence in February. The kids watch less TV. Devin is preoccupied with, coincidentally, a bridge he is erecting between the south end of the dining room table and a windowsill four feet away. His construction materials are manila folders scissored into road sections, duct tape, Q-Tips (guard rails), and string (cables.) He builds tollbooths and a Lego toll-gate that swings up and down. He draws lane lines, pedestrian walkways, and diagonal parking spaces. He brings cars and buses from his room, and creates his own private traffic snarls. Taking into consideration our heightened level of terrorist alert, he stations several army men at the tollbooth and puts another in the flatbed of a pickup truck, spread-eagled, his rifle ready. The kid is like Richard Dreyfuss building the mountain in his living room in *Close Encounters of the Third Kind*. I just leave him alone.

On Friday both kids have playdates at our house, which is so trashed by Hour 3 that I clear everyone out, leading a smoothie run to the Red Hill Shopping Center. Willa's friend Marlena makes an unauthorized detour into the pet shop. Pretty soon all four kids are in there. I ask D.'s little buddy to stop tapping his forefinger against the glass of an aquarium. "That really bothers the fish," I tell him. "Haven't you seen *Finding Nemo*?" While I'm making sure he didn't break any glass, or animals, I see Marlena drop a bunny on the floor. They aren't my kids, but from the way the manager is looking at me, I know that if they break (or maim or kill) something, I'm buying it.

I raise my voice to get them out of the store. In general, however, I do a better job of keeping my temper in check during this second of Laura's prolonged absences. Take the cling peach episode.

With Mom gone, we ingest a few more preservatives, a little more trans fat, some extra sugar. Devin pulls a can of cling peaches off the shelf at Andronico's. "Why not?" I say. Back home, once the can is opened—I start the job, he finishes it—he sticks his hand inside, casting about for fruit, serrated metal edge be damned.

With the aid of profanity, I ask him to remove his hand from the can and pour the peaches into a bowl. He does this with shockingly little spillage. *Now, this is progress,* I am thinking, until I see him pick up the bowl, the better to chug the peach juice, which is practically sugar water, which is Laura's problem with it. But the juice is trapped behind a kind of peach-jam, causing it to rise to dangerous levels. The oblivious lad tilts the bowl still more acutely, until a tsunami of peach syrup washes ashore on his face, saturates his clothes, and pools on the floor.

No use crying over spilled peach juice, I tell him while swabbing the deck with a towel. When the kids screw up, they like to know as soon as possible whether or not I intend to fly into a Bob Knight–like fury. (Not this time.) While I towel, he stuffs peaches into his mouth with both hands. One step forward, two back.

During our conversation that night, Laura tells me she and her six friends had gone out to dinner, then gone skinny-dipping. I tell her about the playdate, the bridge, and our trip to the high school track, Spike and I on foot, the kids on their bikes. For every lap they rode, I paid them a quarter. Willa soaked me for three bucks, Devin for $2.25. The dog and I got a run in.

Laura disapproves. "You shouldn't pay them to do that," she says. First of all, I tell her, that was the only way I was able to get them out of the house. Personally, I thought it was a creative piece of parenting. Secondly, if you want to maintain control over events in the household, then don't abandon it for eleven days. That was a conversation that did not end on a sweet note.

I pine for her the next day, and the three of us say little during a lugubrious dinner, Dad hitting the Chardonnay, Willa immersed in the new *National Geographic,* Devin devouring corn on the cob in his signature fashion, shearing off kernels by holding the cob vertically, then forcing it down onto his mah-jongg-tile-sized lower incisors, as an old-growth redwood is debarked at a sawmill. Sometimes it helps to have an underbite. From the CD player arises the plaintive voice of Lucinda Williams, mirroring my mood as she sings about feeling "so f——in' alone."

"It's her album," Devin concludes, having absorbed the f-bomb. "She can say whatever she wants."

At three minutes to nine the phone rings. With increasingly frantic movements, I search for the headset, which is under some laundry on the bed. I pick up on the fourth ring, but the voice mail has jumped in ahead of me.

It is Laura. It's midnight there, she says, so I probably shouldn't call back, or I might wake the hosts.

The disappointment I feel, missing her call by two seconds, makes me realize how urgently I'd hoped to talk to her, just to tell her about our day. I would have recounted our journey to Old Navy, where we took care of the kids' summer clothes needs. I'd intended to drop it into conversation that I'd washed the station wagon and laid down fresh pea gravel in the side yard where Spike does his business. But I'd missed her, and by the time I speak to her tomorrow it will have been *two whole days* since I spoke with her. Catching a whiff of self-pity, I reflect on how many times I'd left her at home for a week, ten days, two weeks, and didn't think that much of it.

WHEN GOVERNOR LAURA IS AWAY, I FORGET TO GO TO BED. IT IS approaching midnight and I am catatonic before the tube when a late-night commercial comes on hawking the revolutionary Clorox ReadyMop mopping system. It's more than a mop, Jack, it's a mopping *system*. The trigger on this baby directs a three-pronged stream of Clorox floor cleaner into the path of a scientifically designed mop.

To sell this one, the ad agency roped in a couple of real housewives, thickset and earnest. By their Weeble shapes and Kmart-wear, we shall know them as the genuine article, and we shall instinctively trust their testimony.

Earlier in the evening, I'd spent time on my hands and knees scrubbing the kitchen floor. Deeply annoyed though I may have been to discover that neither sweeping nor conventional mopping would lift Spike's dried mudprints off the already hideous linoleum, I did not kick or strike the dog. I accepted the stoop labor as my spiritual practice. Chop wood, carry water—that's what I always say.

Instead of mocking the crappy production values of the ad for the Clorox ReadyMop or the banality of our consumer culture, I find myself thinking, *You know, if I see one of those mops over at Walgreen's, I might just pick it up.*

I'm putting on weight. I'm not as angry as I was during the winter months. I covet a Clorox ReadyMop. Talk about a metamorphosis. Maybe I should have my own construction-paper butterfly.

Once More into the Breach

At Oliver's bookstore in downtown San Anselmo, the theme in the display window is maritime adventure. Titles like *The Endurance* and *My Old Man and the Sea* and *Farther Than Any Man: The Rise and Fall of Captain James Cook* stare out at and, frankly, mock me.

I can hear Shackleton—or Kenneth Branagh, playing him— ask me, "To what exotic ports of call will you be transporting your readers, Mr. Mom? Hearts Desire Beach, scene of your son's last field trip? A meeting of the Parents Club, for riveting discussion of the advantages of replacing the sand in the playground with tanbark? To the table where you stand on chickenstrip day, on the lookout for blackguard second graders who would dare attempt to take two Tootsie Rolls, rather than the allotted one?"

Eat my shorts, Ernest. One need not venture out of one's hemisphere—or home—to find dangerous, frightening locales. One of the jobs I agreed to do when I signed up for this gig was clean the closets, a Herculean labor for which I've set aside several days.

It'll be easier in an empty house. Camp started this week, and it's so tranquil around here, so serene, that I am filled with longing to see my children.

Right. And Shackleton never tired of the taste of penguin. Canon Sports Camp has been an instant hit. Willa made a new friend, a girl named Kim, and Devin . . . Devin likes the snack bar at the pool. Dad doesn't mind the fact that the pool where the kids get picked up is teeming with swimsuit-clad moms, including the Alpha MILF.

The Alpha MILF can be seen poolside, on some afternoons, in a bikini you could fit into an Altoids tin. The Alpha MILF had her children young, is my guess, because she seems different from the other Brookside moms. She seems . . . *firmer.*

The cornerstone of any marriage is honesty, and Laura's and mine is no exception. She knows I will not feel threatened if she confides in me that she finds another man attractive. When we're watching the Giants game, for instance, and Robb Nen comes in to slam the door in the ninth, she unfailingly remarks on how she wouldn't kick him out of bed for eating crackers.

So I had no qualms mentioning to her not long ago that the Alpha MILF has done an admirable job of, well, keeping herself up. "She has," Laura allowed. "But she's kind of got that bad-girl look going."

I nodded in silence, waiting for her to make her point.

My philosophy on scoping women other than my wife is realistic, practical, and based on the *Seinfeld* episode in which

George is caught looking down the blouse of a network executive's sixteen-year-old daughter. "It's like the sun!" Jerry later scolds him. "You glance, then look away."

Discretion is the key here. Without discretion, the fabric of the suburbs begins to unravel. Without discretion, women begin to see you for the pig you are. The Alpha MILF has already busted me a couple of times. I think she noticed me noticing her last spring, after one of our kids' karate lessons. I sneaked a peek at her rack outside the dojo. It happens. Still, I must be more careful in the future. As Goldfinger says to 007, "Once is happenstance. Twice is coincidence. The third time is an enemy action."

IT'S WORK GETTING THEM OUT THE DOOR IN THE MORNING, BUT not as much work as it would be if they dreaded camp, which they do not. The only tension in our house lately has been between Laura and me.

She was pretty much a spectator this morning while I made breakfasts, made lunches, unloaded the dishwasher then partially filled it with the morning's dishes, got a load of wash going, and loaded the kids' bikes, followed by the kids, into the car. Just before I pulled out of the driveway, Laura asked, "Did you remember to pack their swim goggles?"

I had not. Good catch. The mistake is rectified.

"Thank goodness for Mommy!" chirps Willa.

Grrrr.

When she wasn't working hard in New York—it's not easy, coming up with fresh, edgy story ideas, dressing up, and being "on" for editor after editor—she was socializing hard, skinny-dipping with her friends, comparing wax jobs and whatnot. It was the inverse of our normal lives: she returned from her travels spent and in search of sympathy, whereas I, having kept the operation running for eleven days (but who's counting?), didn't want to hear much from her other than "Thank you, thank you, thank you, how can I ever repay you?"

The truth is, by this time I am feeling my oats as a stay-at-home dad. Laura wasn't happy to come home to the sight of a cardboard bridge from the dining room table to the wall. So it was a bit of an eyesore. So it was a little tough on the furniture. (When it finally came down, our duct tape anchorage took a bit of finish off the table, and some paint off the windowsill.) It occupied the boy for hours. Someday when he's an engineer, you'll thank me, I tell Laura.

Superbly competent as she is at teaching me her system, I'm asking Laura to acknowledge that her system isn't the only way to go. I'm a guy. I bring different things to the table, like Capri Sun drinks, Kraft Lunchables, and Klondike Oreos.

While she acknowledges the validity of my point, there remains this uneasiness between us. Let's face it: in her mind, I'm still on probation. She probably thinks I should be going around the house, and the neighborhood, wearing a pin that says TRAINEE. Last night she asked me to make a composed salad, using leftover beef from a gigantic brisket. (While I do the bulk of each week's shopping, Laura enjoys strolling through the farmers' market, where she picked up that brisket. Travis, her "meat guy," is forever giving her deals on beef. I probably need to keep an eye on that.)

Anyway, I mixed everything up—beef strips, potato slices, lettuce, green beans—thinking it should be presented like the Cobb salads I order from room service on the road. "No," Laura said, when I served dinner, "everything is supposed to stay in its own little area. That's why it's called a 'composed' salad."

Fine. We live and learn, and I want credit for what I've learned, what I've accomplished. I didn't see her pulling off a forty-one-act Variety Show. I didn't see her getting a purple bag from Jan Bishop.

And here I am, girding my loins to go in and clean the closets.

I tackle Devin's first. The toys in his closet go into one of three piles: We'll Keep It, We'll Put it in the Rat Room, or We'll Give It to the Poor Kids.

The Poor Kids will be forced to take a pass on these items, as neither Goodwill nor Ritter House is accepting toys. I'll end up carting them to the dump. Devin seems to sense this, and engages me in vigorous debate regarding my categorization of certain playthings. Moved by his impassioned, principled stand on his aircraft carrier—*Throw away my shoes, if you must,* he pleads, *but make room for the carrier*—I relent. The carrier stays.

All things Bionicle are dump-bound, consigned to that special circle of hell in which their parts become all mixed up, Kopaka's mask with Onua's arms with Tahu's codpiece—a hundred plastic joints and limbs scattered on the carpet, never to be sorted out, always to elicit the muttered curses of adults whose bare feet find them in the night. Devin's entreaties on behalf of the jumbled Bionicle parts lack conviction—he hasn't played with them in months—and are easily overruled.

To save face, he plucks an instruction manual from the Poor Kids' pile. "What's the big idea?" he says. "This goes with my Lincoln Logs train set."

My bad. I thought it was Bionicle-related literature.

"I could build a train that goes across town, powered by farts!"

Even as he makes this threat, he is grabbing hold of the top of his dresser. His knuckles whiten, his face reddens, and he breaks sustained, fricative wind. It sounds like the rending of fabric. My expression says, *What was that?*

"Right before I fart," he explains, "I like to *say* something about farts."

"It makes the fart funnier, doesn't it, son?"

"It does."

"I think so too."

At some later date I'll remind him that, droll as we may find it, flatulence has been judged by the outside world to be vulgar and inappropriate. For now, I'm pleased at the closeness we've achieved in these last few months.

Next stop: the hall closet, whose five shelves have become so densely packed that they present a health hazard. The jostling of any item threatens to create a junk slide, a crap-alanche of detritus that will include such breakable items as picture frames, odd light bulbs, votive candleholders, homely pottery sculpted by children, and more. An hour into this job, after extricating such items from the top shelf as three out-of-circulation wicker Easter baskets, a pair of heavy blue-glass candlesticks (either of which might make a suitable murder weapon for the game of Clue, two shelves below), one Accoutrement-brand children's accordion—stashed there, if dim memory serves, when Devin's avant-garde polka-music-from-hell drove the dog to madness—I realize this: I am looking at a two-day job.

Part of it is the sheer volume of shit, and part of it has to do with the dynamic of closet cleaning: the exercise is drastically slowed by examination of items unearthed. The candlesticks, for instance, stood sentinel in front of an old Gyro bike-helmet box that contained not a brain bucket but, rather, fifty or so old cassettes, a virtual playlist for any FM station that hitched its star to the Best of the '80s and early '90s: old R.E.M., Fine Young Cannibals, early Beastie Boys, Talking Heads, post-Wham! George Michaels (go ahead, laugh, but "Faith" had some smoking tracks on it; you know I'm right), Paul Simon's "Graceland," the Psychedelic Furs.

What's in this big envelope? Looks like blown-up color prints of Lisa's Bermuda wedding. Lisa looks radiant as ever in the pictures, particularly when one considers how hard she went out two nights before the wedding. I remember Laura cradling her little sister's head and shouting, to those who had gathered to watch Lisa be sick, "It's not the rum that's making her throw up—it's the *sugar* in the rum."

That was the summer I wore my hair in a ponytail. I'm pleased to have this chance to dispose of some of the photographic evidence of that inexplicable decision. (I cut my hair a month into the following football season. I was finding it difficult to walk into football coaches' offices in the Deep South looking like a waiter at the Sky Bar.)

I wonder what's in this fancy valise, complete with its own tying string? Oooh. It's some of Laura's old poetry. I read a few lines—it's surprisingly good—then put it away. "In the dark of lowered shades" she is kissing some guy's forehead. I'm not sure if she wrote this before or after we got together. Either way, it feels like an intrusion.

We're so caught up in the chaos of the present—getting them signed up for camp, for instance—that I'd all but forgotten about the serious poetry phase Laura went through in college. She's dabbled in poetry since we've been together, but she has had little time for it since we entered our Practical Period, which coincided with the dawn of parenthood.

Lately there has been a stirring in that part of her soul. Jump-starting a career on short notice is always tough. In Laura's case it's been made more difficult by the depressed economy. She's written a few stories over these past few months, but not for any of the magazines she'd hoped to break into. She had a lot of nice interviews in New York, and she came home with a couple of assignments. But she has so much more to give than is being asked of her, for instance, by *Cheez*, a Kraft-sponsored publication, for whom she is composing fifteen "Tips for Teens."

Laura has been doing service pieces like that for eighteen years, and is apt to pull a Sylvia Plath if she has to do many more. While these role-reversed months have been frustrating for her, they've also provided her with a time for reflection— "time to see that I wasn't going in the right direction, in the cosmic scheme," she told me not long ago. Over the course of these last few months, she's decided to change her direction. Her idea is to get some corporate writing—dry, soulless, rela-tively well-paying—and husband her creative energy for the epic novel she is outlining in her head. If that book gets written (if you know Laura, you know it will), the seeds for it will have been sown during the Experiment. That alone will have made the whole enterprise worthwhile.

THE FIRST CASSETTE INTO THE BOOM BOX IS FROM BRUCE SPR-ingsteen and the E Street Band's three-volume *Live 1975–1985*. The Boss has been much in my thoughts of late. On a Wednes-day night in April when I ought to have been at Willa's third-grade concert, I found myself in an SUV with two urologists and a dermatologist. We were headed for the Arco Arena in Sacramento. The day before, I'd returned from Willa's field trip to Miwok Park—the docent, Vera, had looked askance at me when I'd slunk out of her discourse on basket weaving to make a Starbucks run—to a message from my friend Patrick B., who, while not *my* urologist, is a urologist. Would I care to accompany him and some friends to see Springsteen in Sacramento the following night?

Willa forgave me. Before leaving, I baked seven chicken thighs—skin side up, olive oil, a little salt, a little pepper; ninety minutes at 350—and covered 'em with foil. Then I headed to the urologist's office.

I was joining Patrick, his colleague Gary, and Gary's wife, Jody—the "it" dermatologist in our town. "Hey," Jody said to Patrick early in the drive, "I had a patient limp in to see me the other day. You'd done his vasectomy the day before."

At one point, on I-80 near Vacaville, all three of them were on their cell phones, leaving or checking messages. Gary and Patrick were trying to hook up with a fellow urologist at the show. They wanted to do some networking, maybe get the guy to funnel a few patients their way. When the conversation turned to finance, Gary mentioned his and Jody's plan to "open 529 accounts for the kids next week."

By then, one of the questions I'd had earlier in the day had pretty much been answered. I hadn't been to a concert at a stadium-sized venue in a good fifteen years. I'd wondered if anyone would want to catch a buzz. Back in the day, the question would not have been, Should we bring beer? but rather, Will a case be enough? Long before Gary brought up the subject of 529 accounts, I knew I was in for a drug- and alcohol-free evening.

The Boss made us work for it, not coming out until 8:20. On this, the day Saddam Hussein's statue was toppled in Baghdad,

Springsteen's first few songs conveyed uncertainty and darkness: an edgy, acoustic "Born in the U.S.A.," followed by a cover of Creedence Clearwater Revival's old protest anthem "Who'll Stop the Rain"

At one point he asked us, in a polite way, to shut up—"We're gonna get a little quiet for the next few songs"—and the crowd of seventeen thousand–plus fell silent, except for the four drunks behind us. I was surprised and impressed when Patrick, an ex-cross-country runner who is built like . . . an ex-cross-country runner, turned and told them to put a sock in it. Chastened, they fell silent.

Prostate Boy—showing me something!

Later on, during a gospel-influenced buildup to "Mary's Place," Springsteen listed two criteria for a good house party. "First, the music has to be *righteous!*"

Check.

"And second"—he seemed to be looking to his left at this point, looking up at Section 218, at a trio of doctors and their friend in Row C, seats 1 through 4—"You got to get off your asses, people."

So we were up for the rest of the show, through "Badlands" and "Jungleland" and the concussive guitar riffs of "She's the One." I ended up dancing in the aisle during "Born to Run" with the wife of one of the drunks, who was away on a beer run or a piss stop. For the chorus of "Worlds Apart," Springsteen was singing a cappella with his wife, Patti Scialfa.

They look and sound great together. She's his second wife; they've been married twelve years now. Not everyone gets it right on the first go-round.

But I did. I am reflecting on that during closet cleaning. Having moved down to the second shelf, while foraging among such miscellany as Halloween supplies, cheesecloth—what the hell *is* cheesecloth?—a brown bag of Christmas-tree ornaments and a ten-year-old camcorder the size and weight of a rocket-propelled grenade launcher, I locate, then disinter a big red Saks box. Inside are special things, mementos that bring the closet cleaning to another unscheduled halt. Here is an eight-by-twelve photograph of Laura that had been a candidate for the cover of *Parenting.* In the picture, which was shot from behind, she is nude to the waist and holding a three-week-old, still vaguely coneheaded Willa, who told me this morning with an air of weary condescension that if she had time after camp, she would teach me how to copy songs from a CD onto my laptop. I am dumbstruck for a moment, wondering, *How did she get from here to there?*

Here's the announcement we—Laura, I should say—sent out after Willa's birth, and the one that went out following the arrival of Devin. It has fewer flourishes and a more matter-of-fact tone, as will happen with second children. I spent Devin's first night on earth in the hospital lounge, tapping away at a bonus-length story on sports talk radio that was due in the morning.

I hold the birth announcements up to show Laura, who has returned, at that moment, from a shopping trip, but I cannot get a word out before she lights into me. Alas, I deserve it.

Upon attempting to withdraw cash that morning, she'd been informed by the ATM that our mutual account stood at −$801. I'd paid a work-related bill with a thousand-dollar check. But the people to whom the check was written sat on it for a month before cashing it. That threw me off.

Laura is frantic and panicked, ticking off the people to whom we've probably written bad checks. "I *told* you before we started that I would get *really* mad if you screwed up the finances," she says, "and I'm really mad. You are going to have to reconstruct the whole checkbook, entry by entry, until we get this straightened out."

I agree to these terms, nodding dumbly even though I know the account to be in such shambles as to make its reconstruction all but impossible.

So far I've not delved into finances in any depth, for the excellent reason that I never really delved into them in any depth when I was in charge of them. They were a shameful secret, like Dick Morris's sex life, one that I'd hoped to keep hidden forever.

The bills I eventually take care of. If you are a utility or a service and you call and tell me you're about to cut off the cable or turn off the electricity or the phones, I'll send you a check. If you're really insistent, as the PacBell woman was three weeks ago, I'll drive to the payment center and stand in line with the guys cashing checks and slide the money under the bulletproof Plexiglas. We'll get this sorted out.

The checking account is a different story. I can't fix it right away. It's too far gone. I let it get away from me, and there's no getting it back. I have found it too easy to say to myself, after paying with plastic for gas or groceries or dinner on date night, that I will enter the amount in the checkbook when I get home. But sometimes I can't find the checkbook. Sometimes more pressing business commandeers my attention. Not being a complete screwup—just a partial one—I have devised a receipt-storage system, wherein I accumulate receipts at a variety of sites around the premises: in my wallet, on my dresser, and on my desk in the office, in the old coffee pot that also contains pens, pencils, a broken flashlight, a defunct California Academy of Sciences family membership card, and an adapter for electrical outlets in Germany.

Those receipts accumulate fast! You've gotta stay on that! I couldn't, so after a while I stopped trying. I just kept an eye on our balance when I used the ATM, and fooled myself into thinking I had a rough idea of how much was in the account. That worked okay until my friend Tracyn from the Appalachian Extreme sat on that check for a month, then deposited it, thus dropping a Daisy Cutter bomb into the Tora Bora caves of our account.

So I sit there on the bed, surrounded by mementos, the air around me still ringing with the bitter denunciations of my wife, with whom, truth be told, things have been a bit rocky anyway. The next envelope I pull out of the Saks box contains our wedding invitation. A blackout at the San Felipe de Neri Church in Albuquerque moments before the ceremony meant that the musician we'd hired could not play "Ave Maria"—Laura's request—on the organ. Thinking on his feet, the fellow grabbed his guitar and launched into "The Rose." Laura was mortified. She wondered, as she walked up the aisle, if it was possible to put a stop payment on the check we'd already given this guy.

Replacing the invitation in its fifteen-year-old envelope, I cannot hold back a tiny smile. I am in a deep hole, the deepest this year, but I do not despair. A true reconciliation is not in the cards for tonight, or possibly even the night after. But within three nights I will be in her arms again. It is a sure thing. Among the verities these months have taught me is this: it's hard for a woman to resist a man determined to clean every closet in her house.

Vacation

Independence Day is behind us and I have bowed to the inevitable, have made my peace with the fact that I will never fully master this drill. I've decided to do something I'm really good at: forgive myself. No use breaking out the hair shirt over the finances.

Laura has decided that she will take them over before something serious happens—like, say, the bank forecloses on the house. I swallow my ego—and the temptation to shout for joy on the rooftops—and agree that it would be best for our family.

My focus will be on getting as much right as possible for these final weeks of SAHD-ness. We are leaving on a two-week vacation to the East Coast. I'd like to nail this. I want to finish on a high note. I'd like to get through with no major foul-ups.

———

WITHIN TEN MINUTES OF ENTERING THE OAKLAND AIRPORT, WE are surrounded by unsmiling transportation security agents. One of us, it seems, has attempted to transport a dangerous item into the secure area.

The X-ray machine has detected, in one of the remote and hidden pockets of Willa's Tostitos Fiesta Bowl wheelie suitcase (she doesn't know it didn't cost me anything, and I'd appreciate it if you didn't tell her), a snub-nosed, one-and-a-half-inch-long pair of scissors. That's a no-no. The sight of the agent examining the bag, vainly searching for the scissors, is too much for Willa and Laura. They crowd in close, Laura helpfully suggesting places he might look, Willa pulling on the bag's zippers. Finally the agent, a large, perspiring African-American man, says, with annoyance, "Could I just look through the bag, please?"

To the women in my life I say, "He actually does this for a living." To the agent I say, "Welcome to my world."

We're flying JetBlue, which means, BYOF. In addition to picking up Lunchables for the kids, I grilled a bunch of chicken thighs and packed sliced fruit and carrots. Laura isn't happy about the Lunchables—they earn me a brief lecture on the evils of nitrites—but compliments me on the rest of the victuals. She should just thank me for serving as a firewall between her and her issue. She is insulated from their conflicts and demands by me, then by the aisle. She has a very relaxing flight, making good headway in *Brideshead Revisited*.

We rent a midsize car at Kennedy and miraculously find the Long Island Expressway on our first try. Our South Fork destination, the house of our friends Neil and Lorie, is ninety minutes away, and seems to be the cynosure of a gigantic lightning storm that thrills us for the duration of the drive.

Neil Torpey is my oldest—okay, my *only*—college friend. We played rugby together at Colgate and shared an apartment in New York City until I got serious with Laura. I was a wing on the rugby pitch; he was an outside center who didn't pass me the ball very often. Still, the guy has had my back for twenty-two years, and is regarded by my family as the unofficial fifth Murphy brother. While both of us have flourished professionally, Neil chose a line of work in which *flourish* is a synonym for "become seriously freaking affluent": he's a partner at a heavyweight New York law firm. Our children and wives play beautifully together. The last few summers, we've crashed for a week at their house in Quogue, near Westhampton.

It's especially good to see them this summer. For the last year, they've been in Hong Kong, where Neil opened an office for his firm. The kids—even four-year-old Piper—spend the week trying out their Mandarin on us. Dieken, who's Devin's age, tries to haggle with the cashier at the aquarium in Riverhead, as if he is at one of the Asian outdoor markets where he and his sibs have learned to drive a hard bargain.

Usually I'll take advantage of vacation time to get in some hours-long bike rides. This summer, I don't even bother packing up the old steed. Laura has assured me that no such broad workout windows exist for vacationing moms. I've been advised to expect much less leisure time.

Grasping that concept intellectually and forcing my body to rise up off the sofa prove to be two different things. Let me admit that I get off to a slow start on this vacation, too often lingering over coffee, listening to Neil hold forth, for instance, on England's chances in the upcoming Rugby World Cup and its mastery of the "rolling maul," while the women do the work. For the first couple of mornings I look on, seemingly paralyzed, as Lorie cleans the breakfast dishes, as Laura applies the children's sunscreen. I am not being a good wing, not looking for work.

I know better, yet feel powerless not to backslide into old behaviors. I am unfamiliar with the turf—someone else's refrigerator, someone else's cabinets and silver drawer, someone else's dishwasher. I defer to Neil and Lorie when I ought to muster my assertiveness and command, "Sit down. Let me do this."

When I fire up the rented Grand Am and head out shopping, their grocery store, Waldbaums, baffles me. I push the cart aimlessly through aisles that seem too narrow, wondering where they have put the robust produce, the proud, oversized fruits and vegetables. It dawns on me that this is as good as it gets on Long Island. I can't find organic anything. Laura will not be pleased, I think. We are spoiled in northern California.

Part of my problem is that I have fallen prey every morning to the lotus leaves of Gotham, the tabloids. Specifically, the *New York Post,* a guilty pleasure for which we have no analogue in California. How else would we know, were it not for the *Post,* what fallen ImClone founder Sam Waksal had to drink on the eve of being sent off to federal prison (Château Lafite-Rothschild)? Where else might I learn that Chris Martin, frontman for my new favorite band, Coldplay, was arrested in Australia for bashing in a photographer's car window?

One morning, as Neil and I are mesmerized by the Outdoor Life Network, which is airing the Tour de France—Jan Ullrich has attacked on the Col de Tourmalet; now Lance Armstrong is slowly reeling him in—Lorie wonders aloud if we intend to help get the children ready for the beach.

"C'mon Lorie," I say. "We're on vacation."

"Really?" she says. "When's my vacation?"

Touché.

But after a slow start, I start to hit my stride. I figure out where things are in Lorie's kitchen. Neil and I head over to a fish store called Corjay's and pick up some fresh Atlantic salmon. I make—or help make—a couple of nice dinners.

On the fifth day of vacation we are joined by another couple, Jamie and Helene. We all head over to Neil and Lorie's beach club for a spot of lunch. (One hour a week. One lousy extra hour of studying per week, I figure, and my grades might have been comparable to Neil's. One more hour a week with the books, and maybe I'd be in a position to take my friends to my beach club for a spot of lunch.)

The grown-ups sit around a picnic table on a wooden deck over the dunes. The shrieks of our children, playing in the surf under the eyes of three club lifeguards, drift up to us. Sun-kissed and windswept, our women look as if they belong in a Ralph Lauren ad. I should say they *would* appear as if they belong in a Ralph Lauren ad, if they didn't all look so tired.

For a glorious hour we talk about politics, finance, sports, what people are reading, and, of course, our offspring. Jamie and Helene have four boys, including two-year-old twins and a newborn, which little ones are now with a sitter. We spend much time nodding sympathetically at Helene while thinking, *Better you than us.*

Lorie is asked to once again tell the story of the day she noticed a suspicious white powder on her mail and alertly phoned the authorities. Not long after, several policemen in full haz-mat outfits—they looked like space suits, she says—appeared at the door of her apartment on Beekman Place. After several tense moments, one of the officers reported to Lorie, "It appears to be powdered sugar, ma'am," his voice oddly muffled from within his protective suit. "Most likely from some kind of doughnut."

The subject of 9/11 comes up, and people start volunteering where they were on that black morning. Laura and I were at home in California; Neil and Lorie in midtown. Jamie seems conspicuously silent, so I draw him out.

"I was at the World Financial Center," he says. Close enough to see falling bodies. "Some people stood and watched everything, but after the second plane hit, I was out of there." He walked up the West Side Highway and called his wife from a phone booth near the Holland Tunnel. He flagged a cabbie, who told him, "I'm not going downtown."

Neither was Jamie, who remembers that his only thought just then was "Get to your family."

I only met the guy this morning but he feels like a kindred spirit. At the end of this month, the end of this half year, I will not have mastered more than four dishes; I will have made a hash of the finances. (Laura now sits at the kitchen table with our checkbook and bank statements, doing what she calls "forensic accounting"—cleaning up my mess. "You have periods of actual responsibility," she says, not looking up. "Brief periods.") I may have thrown away items that ought to have been recycled, may have briefly misplaced my children or left them on their own when I ought not to have.

Despite those and other shortcomings, I am closer with them now—my children and their mother—than we were last January, which capped a year when I'd spent too much time away. In asking for and getting time off from my job, I am heeding a similar, visceral instinct: Get to your family.

———

AND SO WE DO. AFTER FIVE DAYS WITH NEIL AND LORIE, WE BID our farewells and head for the car. We will drive to Orient Point, then onto the Cross Sound Ferry, which will take us to New London. From there, we'll drive to Rhode Island for another week of freeloading—this time in the home of my parents.

We've already done the good-bye hugs when the kids plead for five more minutes on the trampoline. We relent, although I make a mental note to keep a closer eye on them. On the drive home from the Crazy Dog Diner last night, I'd ended up in the middle seat with Devin and Piper, a gregarious lass with surprising news: "Devin and Dieken showed me their penises on the trampoline!" I'd looked at Devin, who'd stared straight ahead, confirming the report by failing to deny it.

"Dieken's was bigger," said Piper.

"And skinnier," added Devin, at last feeling the need to speak.

As our arrival in Rhode Island nears, Devin increases his repetition of the Question to more than twenty times per hour: "Daddy, when can we go crabbing?" He's been talking about crabbing since we left Rhode Island last year. We tie a paper clip to a length of string, bait the "hook" with a piece of hot dog or chicken, and drop it off the side of Point Dock. In no time, we've got a bucket full of crabs, most of them the size of my children's palms. Devin is the Crab Whisperer: he allows them to scuttle around on his hands, up his arms, on top of his head. Willa enjoys the thrill of the hunt, but she doesn't like the crabs touching her person. Her role is to ensure that the crabs are humanely treated, and ultimately released.

You never know what's going to float their boat. A few days earlier, to give Neil and Lorie a reprieve, we'd taken the LIRR

———

into Penn Station and headed up to the American Museum of Natural History. It went about as well as the trip to Vegas. When we took them to the room housing the dinosaur skeletons, they yawned.

"We have to learn about dinosaurs in school every . . . single . . . year," griped Willa, who could not have been more blasé.

Her brother was no better, asking, "Can we go to the gift shop?"

They were underwhelmed, likewise, by the short film on black holes—"which arise from the death of a single star and contain ten times the sun's mass," we were told. "But supermassive black holes range from millions to billions of times the mass of the sun."

If we wandered too near a black hole, we learned, our atoms would be crushed to "infinite density."

Some of us might just deserve to have that happen, was my feeling on the matter that afternoon. Laura and I worried, for a moment, about our children's lack of wonderment and awe, then recalled their reaction upon entering our hotel:

"Check it out—a chandelier in the elevator!"

"Hey, there's a butt bath in this bathroom!"

"Like in *Eloise*!"

"Skipperdee's pool!"

What it boils down to is that if they think they're supposed to be oohing and aahing, they'll hold their fire. Both of them have a contrarian streak that appears to have been passed down, as I see it, from their mother.

BACK FROM CRABBING, I SHUCK THE CORN FOR OUR FIRST MEAL in Rhode Island. While waiting for the water to boil, I winch myself into a comfortable chair alongside my father. We talk about the kids, his golf game, the Westerly Chorus, to which he lends his voice. Before long, our eyes are drawn to the television. ESPN is airing a segment on what we can expect now that Denver Broncos quarterback Brian Griese has been replaced by Jake Plummer. We watch as if there will be a quiz later on, as if any of this matters.

Between the three hours of sleep—I filed a column for *SI* on the Tour at four this morning—and the packing and ferrying and unpacking and crabbing, I'm kicked in the ass. I could say I deserve some easy-chair time. But the fact is, the women are tired, too, and they aren't sitting down. So I stand.

If I had to distill the lessons of five and a half months into five words, they would be these: Fight the urge to sit.

No one does it better than our hostess. While reading in bed that night alongside Laura, I hear creaking overhead. These are the footfalls of Pat Murphy, cheerfully transporting clean, folded sheets to upstairs guest rooms at 10:35 P.M. "Your mother is an amazing woman," Laura notes, not for the first time.

The wall to our left is covered with framed photographs of my ancestors, black-and-white pictures of grandparents and great-grandparents, a murderer's row of prudes and staunch Catholics, unsmiling in corsets and starched collars, gazing down at the occupants of the bed as if to say, *We trust this is for purposes of procreation.*

Anomalous in that dour crowd is a picture of a twenty-year-old Patricia Reeves, a luminous beauty bearing a tennis racket— a reminder of how I came to be here. My parents met at a tennis tournament in 1955. She was playing; he was freeloading. A problem arose when Rex was asked to be a linesman. Unsure of whether a ball that landed on the line was in or out, my old man took turns. His wretched calls infuriated my mother, who confronted him over the punch bowl at that evening's garden party. He asked her out.

She captained the tennis team and played field hockey at Rosemont College, outside Philadelphia; he was an ex–college football player and marine attending the University of Pennsylvania's Wharton School of Business on the G.I. Bill. The athletic young couple married in 1958 and produced seven children in eight years. (Amy, number eight, followed four years later.)

Rex worked for U.S. Steel, and we moved ten times. Stop number three was Denver. While skiing in 1966, Pat broke her left ankle. The injury required a cast up to her knee, which made it difficult, but not impossible, to shift our bile-green, three-on-the-tree Ford van. Pat worked the brake and accelerator with her right foot, depressing the clutch pedal with a drum majorette's baton. It was resourceful, it was illegal, it was Pat at her quintessential can-do best.

My siblings and I played fifteen sports for 159 teams. (How do I know? Upon request, Pat sat down one evening in 1997 and counted them.) There hung, in the kitchen of whatever house we lived in, a two-by-three-foot calendar. Each day was a box, each box a logistical morass of teams, times, places, and players. A typical mid-1970s summer day, as described by Pat: "Leslie and Lorin's swim meet is across town from Austin's Babe Ruth baseball game, which is forty-five minutes after and two miles removed from Chris's Little League game, which starts concurrently with Gibby's softball game, four fields from where Matt and Mark compete in T-ball. Amy is in a playpen, ready to attend any of the above. Mom just wants a nap."

She coached, she carpooled, she cultivated relationships with nurses and doctors in emergency rooms all over the country. "Our last yard sale featured twenty-four pairs of wooden crutches," reports Pat, who shepherded children through surgery on two hernias, three feet, and seven knees. There were casts and slings for fourteen different fractures. We suspect that in 1984, when my father left U.S. Steel, its medical insurance carrier threw a big bash.

Pat nicked herself up, too. Her arthritic feet, operated on five times, are a gnarled testament to a life of hard work and play. There was that skiing mishap. While cycling one morning (to church, during Lent), she took a spill and broke an arm.

There was nothing life-threatening until 1988. Mark was a senior defensive tackle and cocaptain of the Boston College football team that year. Pat and Rex visited scenic Fort Worth for the Eagles' game against Texas Christian. B.C. lost, 31–17. Driving away from Amon Carter Stadium, they were passed by two cars playing fender tag at seventy-five miles an hour. One car rolled, ejecting a young woman my mother later estimated to be seventeen or eighteen. The girl was a bloody mess. My parents stopped, and Pat cradled her in her arms until the paramedics arrived.

Four years later doctors concluded that this was how Pat had contracted chronic active hepatitis C, a blood-borne disease that, untreated, destroys the liver. She threw herself into research and began typing her legendarily chipper Liver Letters, in which she kept us abreast of her battle with the virus. She invariably signed off, "Love, Pat (The Liver Queen)."

Our queen informed us that the only known treatment for the virus was a biological agent called interferon. For three months, three times a week, Pat injected herself in the thigh with three million units of interferon-alpha-2B. It's a nasty drug that wipes patients out and often makes their hair fall out.

It reflects poorly on my siblings and me that we were disappointed by Pat's subsequent failure to lose her hair. Sure, it would have been a grim reminder of her illness. But it would've been good for a few yuks, too. *Oh, excuse me, Sinead, I was just looking for my mother.*

Twice she appeared to have knocked the virus over the left-field fence; both times it rebounded. "Back to the drawing board!" she would burble. Laura tendered this theory on her mother-in-law's supernatural serenity: "Not that it wasn't a pleasure raising eight of you," she said, "but I think your mother looks upon death differently from most people. She probably thinks, Hey, I'll be able to sit down."

The third time was the charm. On January 3, 1996—four years after she first began to fight the disease—she tested clean, and she has continued to test clean for over seven years. Her doctors consider her cured. The Liver Queen has become the Rally Queen.

Her recovery provoked a range of emotions in her children: gratitude that she'd had access to cutting-edge medical treatment; happiness, that she would live to a ripe old age; and relief that she had not made a widower of their father, a man to whom she serves dinner on a tray every night.

As dearly as we love Rex, my siblings and I are in agreement that, in a perfect world, he will precede her.

ON THE SECOND DAY OF OUR VISIT I CLIMB THE STAIRS TO MY parents' upstairs apartment. (When summer comes, they take refuge up here, welcoming their children and grandchildren with one hand while keeping them at a safe remove with the other.) I find my father seated comfortably in his easy chair. There is a tray nearby, leading me to believe he'd been served breakfast.

He is watching MSNBC. "Look," he says, "they're gonna interview a platoon leader from the Korean War."

This morning marks the fiftieth anniversary of the signing of the armistice that put an end to that war. By this time, the American body count in Iraq is in the three hundreds. "How many did we lose in Korea?" I ask my father.

"Thirty thousand," he says somberly. He saw some of those deaths firsthand. After enlisting in the marines in 1951, he became a second lieutenant in charge of a bazooka battalion. He returned from Korea with Bronze Star and a Purple Heart. He tells the story of sitting in the officers' club the day the armistice was signed, then driving out with a buddy to see a position from which they had been driven back, during the war. "We climbed up on the trench lines," he says, "and saw a bunch of Red Chinese two hundred yards away, staring back at us."

He pauses. "I guess it wasn't the brightest thing to do."

Here is a guy who put his life on the line to arrest the spread of communism. He fought and bled, is what it boils down to, to defend my right to grow up and call your attention to his benign chauvinism and domestic—how to put this politely?— *limitations.*

I'm unsure of when the man last did a load of wash. It's no easy thing, navigating your way through all those stridently colorful bottles and boxes—bleaches, detergents, stain removers, fabric softeners: where to begin?—or the alienating knobs on the machines themselves.

Just because I've never seen him unload a dishwasher in the forty-two years I've known him doesn't mean he doesn't know how to do it.

Let's give him his props: he is a superb gardener and a man

who knows his way around the grill. The following night, Devin and I sit on the deck while Rex peppers the steaks, compressing the pepper into them with the palm of his hand—the kind of steak-prep trick that gets passed from males of one generation to the next, but that somehow bypassed me.

Laid on the gridiron, the steaks sputter and hiss. After a while, Rex deftly seizes both cuts of meat—the tensile strength of this man, clasping two steaks with a single set of tongs!—and holds them on their thin end. He is searing the sides, sealing in, the flavorful steak juices. He knows intuitively when the meat is done, announcing in a casual voice that belies the importance of this moment to the survival of the clan, "I think that should about do it."

We process into the house, Rex on point, holding the platter. It is a walk of glory, the promenade of the provider, who proclaims, not in so many words, *I come bearing the seared flesh that will sustain us until the next successful hunt.* Having prepared the meat so magically, how could this man, why should this man, be expected to do anything else?

Even so, Rex pitches in with the dishes that night. I've been riding him pretty hard about the whole getting-his-meals-on-a-tray issue. I think he may have concerns about getting some bad press.

Such groundless fears. Just because he became slightly petulant when it took longer than he liked for people to be seated—"This meat is getting colder than a well digger's ass," he grumbled—just because his mood further deteriorated when we insisted that the television be turned off during dinner, that's no reason to pile on a decorated veteran.

"It's the Red Sox game," he protested. To review: we haven't been out here in two years, and have probably fifty or fewer dinners left with my father before he rides that La-Z-Boy to his eternal reward. My sister Gibby and her husband, John, are here, as are Neil, Lorie & Co., who surprised us, taking the ferry over on short notice. (There is Kiki, intoning the Mandarin pre-prandial blessing, *"Gong-si! Gong-si! Gong-si!,"* causing all the children in the household to take up the chorus).

Since I've started preparing meals myself, I've come around to Laura's way of thinking about dinner as a social event, a time for conviviality, a mini-celebration. Two days earlier, the *New York Times* had done a Q&A with Carlo Petrini, founder of the International Slow Food Movement. "Eating together and drink-ing together at the end of the day is a sign of friendship or communion," he said. "And when that doesn't exist, it's a sadder, less cohesive society."

Rex isn't boycotting the meal, so much, by keeping the TV on, as he is letting all of us know: "Hey, it's great to see every-body, and I'll try to stay engaged in the conversation. But just in case you people bore me, I would like the option of looking over your shoulders in order to monitor this critical, late-July contest between the Bosox and the Texas Rangers."

His conviction that every dinner is a TV dinner never really bugged me until this week. Since February, these are the sorts of things I've become attuned to. It all ties in with one of the lasting gifts from the Experiment: I have acquired the Sight. It is both a blessing and a burden.

Unlike Haley Joel Osment in *The Sixth Sense,* I do not see dead people. But I see rude people. I saw Neil, for instance, haranguing Lorie for choosing an inopportune moment to install a new belt on the vacuum, rather than simply thanking her for driving to Riverhead to pick up the part. (Love you like a brother, Torps, but you were out of your depth on that one.) I see people sulking because they can't watch a baseball game at the dinner table. I see people sitting at the table, the meal long since over, letting others handle the cleanup. I see unfolded laundry and kitchen garbage bags so full as to be approaching infinite density. I see layers of detritus in the backseat of the Volvo, burrs in the poodle's coat, unswept floors, unwatered plants, ungroomed children.

I see these jobs and, after listening to my brain tick off reasons to put them off, I maybe try to do them. (With the exception of trimming the kids' nails.)

The Sight has done more than open my eyes to What Needs to Be Done Around the House. It has allowed me to appreciate the people who have been doing this work as long as I've known them. It has led to abiding friendships with more than a few moms, and deepened my respect for all of them.

After dinner, I venture into my parents' apartment. Rex has the Red Sox game on. Pat is in her reclining chair, skimming the local paper. I am surprised—not because she is so bright and it is such a flimsy rag. I am surprised because, other than to drive or take meals, it is the first time I've seen her off her feet in five days.

True Vacation

I run four miles to the beach on Saturday. Laura and the kids got tired of waiting for me and drove away. I could not tear myself away from the Tour, which had come down to a time trial in the penultimate stage, with Ullrich lurking just sixty-five seconds behind Armstrong. With both riders on a rainy course in Brittany and the entire three-week race in the balance, Laura announces, "We're leaving now. You can come with us or get to the beach on your own."

I needed a workout anyway. At the first time check, Armstrong was already down six seconds to the German. Gulp. In ensuing time checks, as they powered over rain-slicked streets toward the city of Nantes, he took that time back, then began padding his lead. I was clearing breakfast dishes when I heard the voice of the commentator say, "Ullrich has gone down!"

He'd carried too much speed into a corner and taken out a row of hay bales. And that was the Tour. "Couldn't Lance still lose tomorrow?" Laura asks when I arrive at the beach, sweat-soaked. I explain to her, as I have explained every year since '99, when Armstrong started winning these things, that the final day is largely ceremonial, ending with ten laps around the Champs-Élysées.

Two of my final days as Mr. Mom will be largely ceremonial, as well. Ten days into our vacation, Laura and I are about to take an actual vacation. We are bound for Block Island, twelve miles from the beach we frequent, although on clear days it seems to creep in closer, like Birnam Wood. Laura has reserved a room in the Spring House Hotel—"All we overlook is the ocean," they say—and Pat, bless her soul, has offered to mind the children.

And so we board the ferry at Point Judith and check into the hotel. While Laura finds it wanting in certain respects—"If I'm paying two hundred and fifty dollars a night," she says (and we are), "I don't want a plastic bathtub and plastic cups wrapped in cellophane. And these bedsheets are a polyester blend. That's unforgivable"—we cannot help but unwind.

We awake the next morning away from Them, and it is good, and we do seem to levitate like air-hockey pucks, so light and carefree do we feel, relieved of our precious burdens.

Having rented clunky bikes the first day, we rent a kayak the next. I hadn't expected to take the boat outside of the Great Salt Pond, Laura being an inexperienced paddler. So it is a surprise to hear her suggest, from her perch in the bow, "Let's just take it out in the ocean."

Zigzagging out of the paths of yachts and ferries, we make

for the channel, hugging its right bank so tightly that we run aground, inducing my wife to make her sole annoying remark of the day: "I think we need to be in deeper water."

Then we are out at sea, my bride and I, drinking in the sight of cormorants loitering on the rocks, and gulls wheeling overhead. Staying within a couple hundred yards of shore, we bear north, past stately, weatherbeaten Victorians, gray-shingled and redoubtable.

We hew close to the shore, with the North Lighthouse growing larger in front of us. After three miles or so, we ride a wave ashore, then walk along a beach that is deserted but for the couple that has piloted a small motorboat out here. Without my mentioning it to Laura, I know she shares my feeling that we, who got out here under our own power, own the moral high ground.

Gazing twelve miles due north across Block Island Sound, we think we can make out the beach where our children are playing. Even as we discussed them during the paddle out here—the vast creativity of Willa, the gigantic personality of Devin—I could tell Laura had not begun to miss them a single iota. Escaping them, every so often, is something she takes seriously.

Before getting back in the boat, she pees in the dunes, declaiming with the gusto of the recently emancipated, "I don't care who sees my bare ass!"

Said posterior is barely back in its bow seat before Laura brings up the subject of the finish line. It takes me a moment or two to realize that she isn't talking about a finish line for our journey today or my journey as a primary caregiver but, rather, for a phase in both of our lives.

"I can't believe Devin is almost a first grader," she says. (That would explain her excellent spirits.) "I know a lot of successful women who didn't become successful until their youngest child entered first grade."

I've been forewarned by hard-boiled moms like Karen R. and Lori L. that it only gets worse—that the expectation of more time for oneself, once the children are in grade school, is a cruel chimera, the old receding oasis. Still, there's no denying that D. will be going from three and a half hours a day at school to six. That, as my friends in the football coaching fraternity might say, is a difference maker.

I've talked about how six months in borrowed robes altered me. Between the two of us, Laura may be the more profoundly changed. With time, finally, to take stock of where she is professionally, she's made some audacious decisions. She's forty years old and no longer willing to allow her happiness be determined by a bunch of childless editors at women's magazines in New York.

Always strong and assertive, she has struck me as stronger and more assertive since we switched jobs. She is less inclined then ever to stand for it when I let fly with something snide, some cheap shot. She'll get right up in my face and tell me, "Not okay"—as if I were her third child. She's got a book-writing career on her mind and has never had a stronger sense of herself. I find it attractive. I look forward to the remainder of my journey with this woman in the bow of the boat, this character who doesn't care who sees her bare ass.

First, I need to discuss the remainder of the day's trip with her. Emboldened by her paddling success on the way out, she has suggested an alternate route for the return trip. Rather than hug the coast, Laura wants to follow the rhumb line back to the channel, even though this will mean paddling a mile or so out to sea.

After coming up with several reasons why this is a bad idea— it's choppier and more turbulent out there, with bigger boats making bigger waves; we'll be a long way out if we tip—it occurs to me that we really have reversed roles.

"Let's do it," I say.

So the gray homes grow smaller, the ferries and freighters bigger. A treble-chinned plutocrat passes by, too close and too fast. Instead of swamping us, the wash from his yacht bears us up, then down, then up again, like a carnival ride. While I work to keep my composure, Laura laughs, and her casual attitude toward our predicament makes me wonder if it is a predicament at all.

Halfway to the Great Salt Pond, we come upon an anomalous patch of water flat as a millpond, just beyond which we see some serious chop. It makes me nervous. "This should be interesting," I say as we bear down on the rough water.

"And fun," adds Laura. And of course she is right.

Epilogue

At the end of her book *Fruitful,* Anne Roiphe makes a list of some things she'd like to see happen—things that would improve the lives of families, particularly the women in them. There, between "Change the focus of our concern from the sexual issues to the practical ones" and "Create decent, small, non-bureacratic daycare," is this:

"Bring men into the home."

"Just as we changed the image of the doctor from male to male and female," Roiphe continues, a bit later, "we can change the image of father from outside to inside, from an onlooker to a full partner. . . . Why not? It's worth a try."

Who knew? While cutting the crusts off Willa's sandwiches, I've been on the cutting edge of social change, a foot soldier in the long slog toward happier families in which moms are allowed to use their college degrees, to use their brains, to make some money without it feeling like they're working a double shift every day.

I haven't just lightened Laura's load for six months. This isn't a tax cut that will be revoked by the next administration. I am now equipped to be a bigger help for the remainder of our days together. When I'm home, I'm cooking a couple of nights a week. I'm grocery shopping, laundry folding, floor sweeping— you name it . . . other than anything having to do with finances. Sure, there remains a gap in our standards, so that I will always be doing less than I think I am doing. But every little bit helps. If I am not, like Thomas, a "very useful engine," I am at least a more useful engine than I was. For now, that will have to do.

There was more to the job, obviously, than those chores. About a month after I go back on duty with *SI*, Laura says something that sticks with me. My time in her shoes has left me "more willing to take on the responsibilities of parenting, rather than just the fun part."

She says I finally understand the importance of being the Bad Cop; that I've stopped undermining her, that I'm "growing up as a parent."

I'm also growing out as a parent. I doubt I'll ever get back under 180.

An example of my newfound role: When Willa learns that we've signed her up for soccer, she refuses to play. Even though she improved dramatically in her first season, had a blast, and won a trophy, she decides she would rather read, draw, and play with Bratz than endure this scheduled activity. "Fine," I tell her. "But we're going to walk to the park for your first practice, and you're going to explain to your decision to your new coach."

The coach, a local periodontist named Eric, plays it brilliantly, hearing Willa out, nodding with compassion, explaining that his daughter felt the same way the year before. But she'd decided to go through one practice, just for kicks. If Willa wanted to maybe stick around for this one practice—obviously he didn't expect to see her after that, because she didn't want to play— that would be fine with him.

We leave, she stays. She will play the whole season, emerging as one of the top goal scorers on the team. She has fun and we have fun, watching her confidence grow by the week. It turns out that Willa isn't just a crack student with a voracious appetite for books and a soft spot for animals. She's a pretty good athlete.

Encouraged by this success, I take a similarly hard line later in the month, when Devin is being, as I see it, unreasonably stubborn. He'd received in the mail a charming invitation to a classmate's birthday. Graham is one of his fellow first graders, a delightful child. We RSVP right away. Of course Devin will be there.

"Why did you say that?" D. demands, crossly. "You should have asked me."

What we do not say: "Because if we can clear your ass out of the house for two or three hours on a Saturday afternoon, and all it's going to cost us is the price of Bionicle, you're gone."

What we do say: "Because all your friends will be there. Because there will be cake, and a bouncy, and treat bags."

"I'm not going," he states.

"You are going," I counter, "if only to look Graham and his mom in the eye and explain to them that you've decided you don't want to go to the party."

"I'm sorry, but I don't want to be at this party," he calmly informs Graham's mother the minute we arrive at their house. He repeats the message to Graham on his way out the door.

You win some, you lose some.

FOOTBALL HAS STARTED UP AGAIN, WHICH MEANS I'M BACK ON THE road, and the giant Wisconsin banner is flying from Mr. Finnane's front porch. My man is borderline insufferable for six days after his beloved Badgers upset Ohio State. Wisconsin promptly drops games to Purdue, Northwestern, and Minnesota, and David pipes down.

The Big Ten is brutal this year; the traffic circle, less so. Due largely to the efforts of the indefatigable Gina F., bus service is now available up Butterfield, which has taken a lot of cars out of the circle. Plus, Kandee had signs put up that say PLEASE PULL ALL THE WAY FORWARD. Compliance is high. Flow is markedly improved, which is a good thing. I guess. The truth is, I liked having some thoughtless motorist to despise early in the morning. It vested me with a sense of superiority. It got the juices flowing.

I'm all over the place, as usual: Tuscaloosa, Ann Arbor, Eugene, Dallas, Ann Arbor again. It isn't all football. There is the week I stop in Austin, Texas—on my to the Florida Keys for a swimsuit assignment—for an interview with Lance Armstrong. When I'm home, I'm more involved. When I'm not, it's less of a hardship (for me, at least). After a half year playing Paul Bremer in my own household, a hotel room has never seemed quite so tranquil, or my editors so eminently reasonable.

In mid-October Laura and I attend the wedding of her sister Sarah to a guy named Hunter Hubby, a dashing, metrosexual ex–bike racer with a better wardrobe and better hair than me.

And yet, I like the guy. He shares my passion for the Tour, and he taught me how to use the digital camera Laura gave me last Christmas. He shows me how to store photos in folders on the desktop of my computer. When I'm on the road, I can click on images of our Rhode Island vacation, of the kids atop the mini Eiffel Tower in Vegas, of Devin standing proudly beside the monstrosity that was his cardboard bridge. Thus do I find myself, following solitary dinners in Hyatts and Westins and Marriotts, sitting at a desk as twilight falls somewhere in America, clicking on these images and smiling. Because the children insisted on experimenting with my camera, I am in some of them—partially beheaded, midblink, barely distinguishable behind cavernous nostrils, but inarguably present. The injury to my vanity is outweighed by the satisfaction I get from just showing up in the frame.

I like seeing myself in the picture.

Acknowledgments

This book would not have been possible without . . . stimulants.

Thanks, in that case, to the caffeine vixens at the San Anselmo Roastery and the Java Rama drive-thru in Fairfax. For all you do.

Profound, serious thanks to David Black—agent, advocate, mensch. I am also deeply indebted to Jennifer Barth at Henry Holt, who time and again saved me from myself. Thanks also to the endlessly patient Sam Douglas, who endured my technological shortcomings with good cheer.

To Kandee Adams, David Finnane, and the entire Brookside Elementary School staff and faculty—Jan Bishop and Ruth Leader in particular: I loved seeing you in action. Your passion and professionalism inspire me.

Deborah and Paul Cichocki, Tom Kordick and Amy Knapp, Chris Young and Lisa Hilgers, deep thanks for your hospitality and generosity. Thanks also to Gordon Wright and Ginny Graves—Ginny for the pool, playdates, and sympathetic ear; Gordon for understanding when shopping or cooking supplanted riding or running. G-Man, let's get back on the Bolinas Ridge Trail, ASAP.

To Terry McDonell and David Bauer at *Sports Illustrated*, for green-lighting my hiatus, and to the woman who endured it with class and style and without leaving: Laura Hilgers, MILF among MILFs.

About the Author

AUSTIN MURPHY is a senior writer at *Sports Illustrated*, where he has been on staff since 1984. The author of *The Sweet Season,* he lives in northern California with his wife and their two young children.